T
QUOTABLE
COACH

DAILY NUGGETS
OF PRACTICAL WISDOM

BARRY DEMP

Copyright Notice

Introduction

Have you ever considered coaching (either in your personal or professional life) yet were put off by the commitment of time and money?

The great news is that, with this book, you can be your own coach by drawing on the wisdom of the ages. You don't need any special skills or knowledge, and you only need to find a few minutes to dip in and take out a valuable nugget to apply to your life.

This book is made up of 365 great quotes, each with a short reflection and an exercise to help you apply the words to your life. It isn't designed to be read from cover to cover in one sitting, and you don't even have to read it in order. You might choose to:

- Set aside a few minutes each day (or, if you prefer, two or three times a week) to read each quote and reflect on it. I've designed each one to take under a minute to read.

- Read the book with a group of colleagues at work, discussing the quotes and using the exercises to go further in your professional life.

- Share each quote with your family or friends, perhaps over dinner, and ask for their thoughts and ideas about applying them to your personal life.

- Focus on several quotes on a particular topic of interest (see the index at the back of this book for a list of topics).

I recommend that you find a regular time slot in your day or week for your personal coaching session. This could be first thing in the morning, or last thing at night; it could be during your lunch hour or in the parking lot before you drive home from work. Whatever time you choose, make this coaching part of your regular routine.

About the Author

My name is Barry Demp, and I'm a business and personal coach based in Troy, Michigan. I've coached more than 1,000 people over 20 years, and am a Master Certified Coach (MCC) with the International Coach Federation (ICF).

I work with executives, business owners, and high-potential professionals to help them significantly increase their productivity, profitability, and life balance.

My customized coaching programs support businesses of all sizes, from small entrepreneurial ventures to mid-sized and large organizations. I also work with coaches, consultants, and professionals in transition looking to start and grow their own businesses.

For the past two years, I have been sending out a daily quote (Monday–Friday) to readers of "The Quotable Coach", a website with a free email subscription. Over one thousand people from all walks of life throughout the world have been benefiting from this free coaching.

If you are not already receiving these emails, just visit, www.thequotablecoach.com and enter your name and email address in the sidebar.

You can find out more about me and my coaching philosophy on my website, www.dempcoaching.com.

My wife, Wendy, and I have been married for 35 years and have raised two wonderful children, Dan and Rachel.

#1: "Your vision will become clear only when you look into your heart. Who looks outside dreams; who looks inside awakens."

– Carl Jung, Swiss psychiatrist and psychotherapist

As a former science teacher and professed watcher of the Discovery Channel (and TV shows from my youth such as Mr. Wizard), I have always been fascinated by exploring new worlds beyond my reach.

During my childhood, I even dreamed of one day being an astronaut and visiting the moon and the planets. As I aged and pursued adventure, personal growth, and my career in coaching, I found a new excitement in taking more frequent journeys within my mind and my heart – all without the assistance of a rocket.

Exercise:

Consider engaging in your own inner journey daily, through a practice of your choice such as meditation, prayer, journaling, and the reading of insightful or thought-provoking books or blogs.

#2: "You're more likely to act yourself into feeling than feel yourself into action."

– Jerome Bruner, American psychologist

Do you remember times when, as a child, your parents asked you to do something a bit unpleasant? You know, take out the trash, clean your room, do your homework.... If you're like many people, you probably said, "I don't feel like it."

Today, we experience numerous areas of our lives where the same words prevent us from eating healthy foods, getting proper exercise, and yes, doing those pesky chores.

As a coach for over 20 years, I've observed that people of action – deliberate, habitual, and massive action – seem to consistently feel better and have more energy than those who do their best to conserve their efforts.

Exercise:

For the next week, create multiple Post-it® notes with the famous Nike phrase, "Just do it" and see if you catch the positive, energizing momentum available in an action-packed life.

#3: "People are anxious to improve their circumstances, but they are unwilling to improve themselves. They therefore remain bound."

– James Allen, English philosopher and writer

Do you play the lottery? Are you a wishful thinker? Would you like many of your life's circumstances to change for the better? Do you believe in luck? As a highly optimistic person, I tend to live on the sunny side of life, where I not only hope for the best but also work to create my own luck.

Exercise:

Consider picking up the book, *Outliers: The Story of Success* by Malcolm Gladwell, to explore many surprising insights into the world of success and how the hard work of improving ourselves is a fundamental key to extraordinary living.

#4: "It's not what you've got, it's what you use that makes a difference."

– Zig Ziglar, American motivational speaker

Time management is one of the top priorities for people entering a coaching relationship. We all have 24 hours a day, which would seemingly put us all on a level playing field. Zig Ziglar suggests that some of us simply make far better use of our resources (e.g. time) than others.

Think of time as a currency, where certain activities are worth nothing, some are worth a little, and others are worth a lot.

Exercise:

What differences can you make today in how you spend your time?

Which resources – other than time – can you use more fully to make a bigger difference with your days? Consider love, creativity, energy, and even money as possible resources to explore.

#5: "Don't stumble over something behind you."

– Seneca, Roman Stoic philosopher

Where do you live? You may be thinking about your city, country, and state – that's not what I'm talking about here. I'd like to suggest that we all live in our thoughts, regardless of our physical locations.

With this in mind, how often do your thoughts go to past events and experiences that were negative and upsetting? As humans, we have the ability to instantly travel back in time, to revisit and yes, stumble over these same events along with all their limiting feelings.

Exercise:

Imagine that you are born with an installed-at-the-factory time machine that has three settings: past, present, and future.

How can you, through greater self-awareness and intentionality, limit your negative journeys backwards to maximize your living in and experiencing of the present – and perhaps occasionally venture forward into the delightful possibilities of the future?

#6: "Our job is the excuse through which we get to love people."

– Panache Desai, American spiritual writer

www.panachedesai.com

What percent of your life do you spend engaged in work? For the sake of this quote, I'm going to define work as our vocation, or the way we earn a living.

If you work Monday through Friday, a minimum of eight hours a day, work represents approximately one fourth of your life. If the song lyrics from the Beatles tune are true, and *all you need is love*, or *love makes the world go round*, then perhaps Desai is really on to something.

Exercise:

How can you view your daily work efforts as an act of love, contribution, and generosity, instead of something to get through on the way to your weekend?

#7: "The wise man questions himself; the fool, others."

– Henri Arnold, American cartoonist

One of the greatest tools in a coach's toolbox is the question. For the purpose of this example, I'm going to narrow the type of questions to only open-ended ones. Questions that begin with *who, what, where, when, why,* and *how* provide depth and significance, often reaching new levels of awareness and insight.

I disagree with Arnold that only fools ask such questions of others: after all, I'd be calling all coaches fools! I do however believe that when coaches also ask these same questions of themselves, they often enhance their own development considerably. Arnold might say that a coach without their own internal or external coach is a fool.

Exercise:

Pay attention to the types of questions you and your colleagues, friends, and family members ask one another during the day. See which questions most enhance one another's journey toward wisdom.

#8: "The hallmark of excellence, the test of greatness, is consistency."

– Jim Tressel, American football coach

The pursuit of excellence is no accident. Greatness has never been achieved by anyone overnight. Explore the lives of people who demonstrate brilliance in their fields, and you will find people who, with passion and commitment, make consistent efforts toward their goals.

Every great journey begins with the first step, but we only arrive at our destinations by taking the next, and the next, and the next.

Exercise:

Read an autobiography of someone you admire and see what it took for them to succeed. Google your favorite business leader, athlete, or performer to discover how they got where they are today.

Where could you be even more consistent in your effort to quickly and completely realize your priority goals?

#9: "Success in life comes not from holding a good hand but in playing a poor hand well."

– Denis Waitley, American motivational speaker

www.waitley.com

Have you ever watched the World Series of Poker on television – you know, where the winners walk away with millions? If you have, a notable thing about these tournaments is that the viewer actually sees all the cards of all the players.

Rarely does the winner always get the very best cards. Almost always, the winner is the person who makes the best of the cards they are dealt.

Exercise:

If your life was a game of poker, where your five cards included such areas as work, family, health, faith, and community, how could you make the most of these to always have a winning hand?

#10: "Every problem introduces a person to himself."

– John McDonnell, American track coach

What are your current problems, challenges, or places in your life where you are stopped in your tracks? What is your current situation that has you see these issues as problems? If some hypothetical super-person with capabilities and capacities beyond your own was faced with a similar situation, would these issues be a problem for them?

Exercise:

Consider your current problems as an opportunity to become more aware and clear about your own limiting beliefs, perspectives, and perhaps capabilities.

Consider ways to expand your capacities and view yourself as a super-person who easily tackles such matters.

#11: "God, grant me the serenity to accept the things I cannot change, the courage to change the things I can, and the wisdom to know the difference."

– Reinhold Niebuhr, American theologian and ethicist

Serenity is not something I see much of these days. Life seems to be in constant overdrive.

If the world around is moving too fast and you can't keep up, find the capacity within yourself to slow down, recover your energy, and reset your personal metronome.

Exercise:

Whatever we resist persists. What can you do to accept and allow that which you cannot control? The weather and traffic come to mind.

Where can you tap into your intentions to change things that are changeable? Your health and fitness and personal relationships may fit into this category.

#12: "Concentrate all your thoughts upon the work at hand. The sun's rays do not burn until brought to a focus."

– Alexander Graham Bell, Scottish inventor

When I was very young, I remember using a magnifying glass to focus the sun's rays and burn small holes in a piece of paper. Did you ever do the same?

With this idea in mind, I became interested in the concept that greater focus is also the source of greater achievement. In his book *Outliers*, Malcolm Gladwell establishes that it takes 10,000 hours of focused practice to achieve personal mastery.

Exercise:

What must you do less of (or stop altogether) in your life, so you can start or do more of other focused activities? Consider what matters most to you on your journey to personal and professional excellence.

#13: "The most important single ingredient in the formula of success is knowing how to get along with people."

– Theodore Roosevelt, 26th American President

What man or woman do you know who truly stood alone and had a successful life? Even that archetype of the rugged, independent individual, John Galt in Ayn Rand's *Atlas Shrugged,* seems to be missing the vital component of community and quality relationships.

Quality relationships at home, at work, and in our communities are a vital catalyst in making things work.

Exercise:

What do you observe when people do not have the ability or the desire to get along with others? What specific relationships in your world need your best efforts to create the shared successes you desire?

#14: "If we were to do all we are capable of doing, we would astonish ourselves."

– Thomas Edison, American inventor

What are two or three of your greatest personal achievements? What percent of your total potential did it take for you to achieve these breakthroughs?

Many of us are aware of the story of how Roger Bannister broke the 4 minute mile, and how in the following few weeks, dozens of others did the same.

Look at other achievements in our society in entertainment, science, and business, to see what it took for people to reach their goals.

Exercise:

What are your unique abilities and talents? What invisible barriers must you break to astonish yourself, and how are you going to break them?

#15: "The greatest good you can do for another is not just to share your riches, but to reveal to him his own."

– Benjamin Disraeli, British Prime Minister

I am often asked to share my perspective on the fields of consulting, mentoring, and coaching as a way of supporting others in moving forward. In doing so, I like to distinguish an inside-out contribution from outside-in efforts.

Masterful coaching emphasizes that the majority of the answers and potential lie within the client. As we help them discover their own answers and potential, the lessons learned stick far better than any outside-in concept.

Exercise:

In the multiple roles you may play as a parent, friend, colleague, and business person, how can you reveal the riches in others?

Who in your life will do likewise, bringing out more of the best in you?

#16: "The tests of life are not meant to break you, but to make you."

– Norman Vincent Peale, American minister and author

When we engage in sports, we often test our strength, cardiovascular capabilities, and even our flexibility. When we do so, we grow and become more fit.

The way that the coaching process works is related to this: the idea of learning through experience. When we take on a challenge or pass a test, we become stronger and more capable.

Exercise:

What are the personal and professional obstacles and challenges that are facing you and asking you to be better, faster, stronger, smarter, and wiser?

What tests are you facing that, once you pass them, will help "make" you?

#17: "Do what you can, with what you have, where you are."

– Theodore Roosevelt, 26th American President

Many of us are waiting for the perfect time, the perfect person, and for all the stars to align before we take action, and before we will be happy. Even if a perfect situation comes up occasionally, it never seems to last. What then?

Roosevelt was both a visionary and a realist, charting the course to a better future while still taking into consideration the reality of our daily lives.

Exercise:

Look at the day ahead of you. What can you do with what you have and where you are?

Take action based on this insight and you will likely surprise yourself.

#18: "I firmly believe that any man's finest hour, the greatest fulfillment of all that he holds dear, is that moment when he has worked his heart out in a good cause and lies exhausted on the field of battle – victorious."

– Vince Lombardi, American football player and coach

When my daughter Rachel was young, she loved to dance. In fact, she became very good as a member of one of the top dance studios in the country. Each time I dropped her off for practice, I said, "Do your best, and have fun!" The result was her being on the winning team for the national dance championship for her final three years in high school.

When she did her best and gave her all, regardless of whether she won or lost, she was victorious.

Exercise:

Where in your work or your personal life could you work your heart out for a cause and realize your finest hour?

#19: "Experience is a hard teacher because she gives the test first, the lesson afterwards."

– Vernon Sanders Law, American baseball pitcher

My first career was as a science teacher in Philadelphia, Pennsylvania. Those who know me, know of my passion for learning. Throughout all my education and the process of educating others, I found that very few lessons really stuck unless they were combined with some experience, such as a lab experiment.

When we see and hear, then act on what we learn, we internalize a lesson and it sticks.

Exercise:

What lessons are there to be learned from the day-to-day tests you are taking?

What experiences can you engage in to speed up the learning process?

#20: "Do not wish to be anything but what you are, and try to be that perfectly."

– St. Francis de Sales, French Roman Catholic Saint

Envy and jealousy are traits that rob us of our power. When we focus on the qualities and characteristics of others, we often pine for what we feel may be missing or lacking in ourselves. Personal appearance, physical abilities, and intellectual capacities are just a few such examples.

Instead of wishing to be someone else, what if we fan the flames of our own passions and unique abilities to become our best future self?

Exercise:

What if it was all about the journey within – a perfect-fitting life which was intended all along?

What would be possible if you were perfectly yourself?

#21: "Nothing ventured, nothing gained."

– Anonymous

I think I may have heard this quote or similar ones more than just about any others. If we think about the word "adventure" (closely related to "venture"), we can see how many of us desire more of it.

Think about your last trip to a new destination, a visit to a new restaurant, an exotic food that you tried for the first time, or even a new person you met.

"New" is one of the most provocative words of our time. Sadly, most of us only venture out on holidays, weekends, or other special occasions.

Exercise:

What do you have to gain from venturing out on a daily basis? Where will you begin today?

#22: "Our doubts are traitors, and make us lose the good we oft might win by fearing to attempt."

– William Shakespeare, English playwright

I had a hard time reading Shakespeare in high school – I just didn't quite get it. Maybe it was my impatience or perhaps I can blame my English teacher!

For me, this quote is about fear and how it stops just about all of us in our tracks. Perhaps if we really focus on the good we wish to do, we'll find that secret life lever that will have us try, leap, and attempt, in spite of our fear.

Exercise:

Where is fear keeping you from the good you might do? Where can you find the courage to overcome this fear and make the attempt?

#23: "Keep away from people who try to belittle your ambitions. Small people always do that, but the really great make you feel that you, too, can become great."

– Mark Twain, American author and humorist

Many people have a strong need to be *right* and to make others with different beliefs *wrong*. In fact, some people get a huge payoff from belittling others, and do not see the high cost they pay in dysfunctional relationships and toxic communities.

When we make a small but fundamental shift to a "try it on" attitude, we can find the good and value in what others think and have to say.

Exercise:

Who have you been making wrong or belittling lately? How will you take responsibility for that relationship? By looking for what's great about the other person, you will likely find your own greatness.

#24: "Kind words can be short and easy to speak, but their echoes are truly endless."

– Mother Teresa, Indian Nobel Peace Prize winner

If you too are fond of quotes, you will most likely agree that words are powerful.

The book *Power vs. Force: The Hidden Determinants of Human Behavior,* by Dr. David Hawkins, demonstrates that kindness and love resonate at the highest possible frequencies. When we stand for something and others stand with us, we create an unbreakable human bond that can stand any test.

Exercise:

Notice the words that you and others use. By using a greater number of positive words – and fewer negative ones – you add to the resonant echoes that will last and endure.

#25: "When the student is ready, the teacher will appear."

– Buddha, Indian spiritual teacher

The phrase "perception is reality" seems to suggest that what we perceive, and how we perceive it, makes something real. What if we don't perceive an issue, a challenge, or a lesson to be learned, simply because it is invisible to us?

As a student, we first must see a situation and determine that there is value, opportunity, or benefit in it. Only then is there the potential to hear the teachers and see how they might assist us in capturing the lesson.

Exercise:

Where are you stopped or stuck in your life? Where are your efforts being thwarted?

To whom could you go with this challenge to determine your readiness and receptivity to the lesson?

#26: "When I let go of what I am, I become what I might be."

– Lao Tzu, Chinese philosopher

We all love to be right, to have the correct answer, to know the truth – we think we will then find clarity, stability, and even peace of mind. But what if we are being "right" about ourselves and we have defined ourselves into a safe and limited box?

Defining something limits it. Perhaps, instead, we could distinguish ourselves and open up the possibility of who we could be.

Exercise:

How and in what ways can you rediscover yourself, by releasing yourself from self-limiting beliefs?

If you find this difficult, ask a family member or a close friend for their perspective.

#27: "A man should conceive of a legitimate purpose in his heart and set out to accomplish it."

– James Allen, English philosopher and writer

Life purpose, making a difference, and living a meaningful life are fundamental to happiness.

How can you find your purpose and life direction? How will you know when you are heading the right way, and when you're getting close to arriving?

Exercise:

List your top 20–30 core values.

Cut this list in half, and then in half again, to get to the *real* core.

Next, create a life vision statement, using all of the final list and perhaps most of the second list of values. "Wordsmith" this vision until you feel it is 100% you.

Use your vision statement as the context to inspire your actions in every area of your life: it can help you become happier and more fulfilled.

#28: "As human beings, our job in life is to help people realize how rare and valuable each one of us really is, that each of us has something that no one else has – or ever will have – something inside that is unique to all time. It's our job to encourage each other to discover that uniqueness and to provide ways of developing its expression."

– Fred Rogers, American TV host (*Mister Rogers' Neighborhood*)

When my children were very young, Mister Rogers was a show we often skipped in favor of Rugrats or Sesame Street. I regret that I rarely watched an episode – if only I knew he had so much to say.

What parent doesn't want to help and encourage their children to discover their own unique abilities, and to make a contribution to the world?

Exercise:

What actions will you take by bringing a little "Mister Rogers" into your heart and home?

#29: "The best way to find yourself is to lose yourself in the service of others."

– Mahatma Gandhi, Indian independence leader

We've all heard many similar quotes that speak to this truth, such as "givers gain" or "shift your life from success to significance." I really like the idea of losing oneself in a good way, in order to find our flow, our true north, and our purpose.

When I give, I grow. I feel like I'm living a more expansive and true life. When I get, I feel good, yet it's not the same.

Exercise:

Where can you serve and both lose yourself and find yourself at the same time?

#30: "Good timber does not grow with ease; the stronger the wind, the stronger the trees."

- J. Willard Marriott, American entrepreneur and businessman

I like to go to my health club in the morning to keep fit. It cleans out my mental and physical cobwebs and gets my day off to an energized start.

A key component of my fitness journey is to push myself in areas of strength, cardiovascular fitness, and flexibility. When we push the limits a bit beyond our comfort, we come back the next day stronger and more capable.

The personal growth and development efforts that seem to make the biggest difference are the ones which test and challenge our "timber."

Exercise:

Where in your personal and professional life can you lean into the wind and find yourself better off through the process?

#31: "Happiness cannot be traveled to, owned, earned, worn, or consumed. Happiness is the spiritual experience of living every minute with love, grace, and gratitude."

– Denis Waitley, American motivational speaker

www.waitley.com

Similar to the quote, "The best things in life are not things", this statement points to the idea that happiness, to a large extent, is an inside job. The work of building extraordinary relationships with others, our creator (or higher power), and ourselves, is well worth pursuing.

The depth and full richness of the words *love, grace,* and *gratitude* seems to be infinite and enduring, whereas the "real" world is finite and limited.

Exercise:

What efforts, practices, and habits can you pursue and expand to enhance your happiness and your spiritual experience of living?

#32: "You can't help someone get up a hill without getting closer to the top yourself."

– H. Norman Schwarzkopf, American general

When I was a young boy, my mother would always tell my older sister to take me with her when she visited her friends. I liked being with the big kids, and I really liked feeling included.

Today, I focus much of my life on helping others grow both professionally and personally. Through this process, I've had the great fortune of meeting many wonderful people, and have gained much satisfaction through my efforts. I also found that I too got "closer to the top" in the key areas of my own life.

Exercise:

Where could you advise, mentor, or coach others in your life? In what ways can you expect to benefit through your generosity and care?

#33: "In the confrontation between the stream and the rock, the stream always wins – not through strength, but through persistence."

– Buddha, Indian spiritual teacher

In my earlier years in school, most teachers would have described me as an average to good student with a bit of an attention problem. But in the eighth grade, and continuing through high school, I found a magic quality that I have used throughout my life. It's been a key to my successes.

I realized, through standardized testing such as the Iowa Test and SAT, that I scored in the average to good range – yet in the actual world of achievement, I could simply outwork others to achieve what I wanted.

Exercise:

Where can you apply the power of persistence to outwork others and achieve your goals?

#34: "It isn't the mountains ahead to climb that wear you out, it's the pebble in your shoe."

– Muhammad Ali, boxer and philanthropist

www.ali.com

We all sometimes sweat the small stuff. We often make mountains out of molehills, magnifying issues of little or no importance into giant obstacles and barriers.

How can you keep the small things small, or even find a shrink ray to turn mountains into molehills?

How can you bring a greater perspective to the world around you, so you don't major in the minors of life?

Exercise:

What issues are you blowing out of proportion right now? What do you need to think and do in order to shrink these down to size?

#35: "And in the end, it's not the years in your life that count. It's the life in your years."

– Abraham Lincoln, 16th American President

Are you a quality person or a quantity person? Would you rather have a single scoop of premium ice cream or a half-gallon of the store brand?

We've all heard stories of people who lived into their 90s or even to 100, or about a marriage lasting 60 years. Were they quality years?

Consider which things, experiences, and lessons along life's journey make it a quality one for you.

Exercise:

What do you need to start doing, or do more of, to make each moment a premium moment?

What can you stop doing, or do less of, to make room for the added life in your years?

#36: "If I am walking with two other men, each of them will serve as my teacher. I will pick out the good points of the one and imitate them, and the bad points of the other and correct them in myself."

– Confucius, Chinese philosopher

I have a passion for learning and personal growth. My personal antenna and receiver are always on high alert to the knowledge, wisdom and behavior of others.

One of my favorite questions to ask coaching clients is, "How would you describe your best future self?" If they are unclear about the meaning of this question, I often suggest that they identify the qualities of the people they admire – such as integrity, courage, loyalty, and enthusiasm. They can also identify the qualities that they least admire in others – such as greed, dishonesty, arrogance, and pessimism.

Exercise:

Who are the people that can help you discover and develop your best future self? What are their qualities (good or bad)?

Where can you begin your future journey today?

#37: "There is nothing noble in being superior to some other person. The true nobility is in being superior to your previous self."

– Hindu proverb

We live in a competitive world. Just look at sports, politics, even war. We seem hell-bent on defeating others, even to the point of death.

Rarely is there any nobility in this. Is it noble to stand over your vanquished foe and think, "I'm better than you, I'm a winner, and you're a loser?"

This proverb suggests that there is honor in rising above our primary adversary, ourselves – to be smarter, stronger, more courageous, and more loving. The effort to rise above our previous, more limited, self is noble and no one is made smaller through the process.

Exercise:

In what areas of your life are you committed to becoming superior to your previous self?

#38: "Not everything that is faced can be changed, but nothing can be changed until it is faced."

– James Arthur Baldwin, American author and activist

Like most people, I do a lot of thinking about the world: about what I like and about what I don't like. This includes thinking about myself. Thinking is a starting point for changing something in our world and in ourselves.

As Baldwin suggests, not everything can be changed. Rather than seeing ourselves as weak or powerless to change things, we must move beyond thinking to acting on our commitments. We need to act, alone or together, to change the things that we can.

Exercise:

Where in your world can you move beyond merely thinking about change and instead face it head-on?

#39: "Go to the people. Live with them. Learn from them. Love them. Start with what they know. Build with what they have. But with the best leaders, when the work is done, the task accomplished, the people will say, 'We have done this ourselves.' "

– Lao Tzu, Chinese philosopher

I have been a student of leadership for most of my adult life. I've always been fascinated by how leaders generate "buy-in", alignment, and loyalty, and create a shared vision. Lao Tzu's quote points to something critical about leadership: people are most likely to "buy-in" when they have been actively involved in the creative process.

When people see their own ideas and fingerprints on the work, they have a sense of ownership that feels true and genuine.

Exercise:

Where in your work, family, and community can you draw on others to create the futures you desire? As long as you get there, who cares who gets the credit?

#40: "It's not what we eat but what we digest that makes us strong; not what we gain but what we save that makes us rich; not what we read but what we remember that makes us learned; and not what we profess but what we practice that gives us integrity."

– Francis Bacon, English philosopher

Stickiness and sustainability are words that describe an enduring quality of something. A good example of a lack of stickiness is a New Year's resolution: 95% of resolutions fail.

What factors help us digest, save, and remember the important lessons to make our intentions truly stick? The development of good habits appears to be a key to sustainability.

Through consistent practice, we develop the muscle memory to incorporate these ideas and behaviors into our DNA. The things we consciously want become unconsciously incorporated into our very being.

Exercise:

What two or three habits would make the biggest difference in your life? How could you take action to develop these over the next three to six months?

#41: "How far that little candle throws his beams! So shines a good deed in a weary world."

– William Shakespeare, English playwright

What if we look at ourselves as candles – or for a modern twist, light bulbs? What if good deeds and acts of service are examples of turning up the wattage to shed more light in areas of shadow or darkness?

Exercise:

What areas of your life (or the world) need greater illumination? What are your personal beams of light that you can share with your world to make it brighter and a little less weary?

#42: "Change the way you look at things and the things you look at change."

– Wayne Dyer, American self-help author

We have all heard the phrase, "Perception is reality." But what if we are only our perception and there is no fundamental reality?

One way to test this idea is to see if any reality can exist if no one perceives it. If a tree falls in the woods ... you know the rest.

I'm not really interested in discussing semantics, but in discussing the practical implementation of ideas. Do they work and are they applicable in our world?

Look at great thinkers like Einstein and Edison for similar wisdom to Wayne Dyer's: what we see as problems can be opportunities. Failure can be just another way not to do something.

Exercise:

Look at two or three difficulties you're currently facing in a more optimistic, creative, and novel way. How can you change them simply by changing the way you look at them?

#43: "You cannot dream yourself into a character; you must hammer and forge yourself one."

– James Anthony Froude, English historian

We sometimes hope for a quick-fix that will resolve all our problems, and dream of how our future lives would look. If only we could find that magic bullet.

Dreaming is important. Having a vision is important. But nothing can come to pass without the work it takes to realize our dreams.

The great leaders and people of our time had dreams and shared their visions. To realize those visions, though, they all worked hard, and put in tremendous effort, usually over many years. These people of character have the bumps, bruises, and calluses to show for it.

If you find something of extraordinary value and meaning in your life, and pursue something you truly love to do, you will most likely enjoy the process.

Exercise:

What do you envision and dream about the world that would be worth, perhaps, a lifetime of hard labor?

#44: "Learn from yesterday, live for today, hope for tomorrow."

– Albert Einstein, German American theoretical physicist

As humans, we have a unique capacity to think and to interpret our world. In this regard, we are also time travelers: we can imagine the beginning of time and the Big Bang all the way to, perhaps, the end of our universe.

Let's get real for a moment. This is not what we actually do on a daily basis – except for theoretical physicists. We do, however, visit the past often and, fortunately or unfortunately, re-live it. We often live in the future of possibilities and lose sight of what's right in front of us.

Exercise:

How can you use the lessons of the past to live a more fulfilling life today?

How can your hopes and dreams for the future help you take action today to realize your tomorrows?

How can you savor each and every moment of today as a glorious bridge between the past and the future?

#45: "Be who you are and say what you feel, because those who mind don't matter and those who matter don't mind."

– Dr. Seuss, American children's author

Be authentic. "To thine own self be true." What if people don't like us, or even reject us? There has never been a person who pleased everyone. The best we can do is to please first ourselves and then those in our lives who truly matter.

You can stop being a chameleon, constantly trying to change in order to please those around you. In fact, it is the natural human state of things to become more of who you truly are.

Exercise:

Determine what you value, what really makes you tick, and your fundamental beliefs – and shout them from the rooftops. The people who matter will pick up your signal, and those who don't were never really tuned in to begin with.

#46: "You cannot talk your way out of something you behaved yourself into."

– Stephen Covey, American self-help author

Actions speak louder than words. They are all we really have to make our dreams of a better future become our reality.

Consider a business leader who talks about his core values and corporate vision, yet is seen by his colleagues to act inconsistently with these. Consider the individual who is constantly discussing his interest in health and wellness, yet is often seen making unhealthy eating choices and is rarely seen engaged in physical activity.

Exercise:

Where in life can you bring greater alignment between your actions and your words?

To whom besides yourself will you make these promises, and what added support will be required to ensure this new level of personal accountability?

#47: "Remember to pick something up when you fall."

– Unknown

We have all heard that experience is the best teacher. Many experiences do not provide us with success on the first attempt. Consider a baby trying to take its first steps, a child learning to read a book or ride a bike, a new leader speaking in public to a large group, or an adult learning a new language.

Having a "beginner's mind" and a hunger for the lesson offers us the opportunity for value even in adversity.

Exercise:

Where did you fall down today, this week, and this month? And what did you pick up when you stumbled?

#48: "Nothing happens unless first a dream."

– Carl Sandburg, American poet and author

A dream, a vision, a goal, an objective … these are all words that convey a view of the future. When we envision the future, it seems that a magical attractive power begins to pull us toward realizing it.

Without this first thought of what we want to see, we are left exactly where we are – with something neither good nor bad unless we make it so. However, the moment we think about, imagine, and envision a future, we find the courage and ability to pursue and reach our destiny.

Exercise:

What are your personal and professional dreams?

How can you exercise your capacity to envision your future, and use this to enhance your world?

#49: "To succeed in life, you need three things: a wishbone, a backbone and a funny bone."

– Reba McEntire, American musician and actress

www.reba.com

Many of the quotes I've included in this book discuss the benefit of vision and hard work to help you on your journey through life. I like the added element here of having a funny bone, or a sense of humor, as we navigate this journey.

I personally need to take life a bit less seriously – to be more playful and light-hearted and to have a whole lot more belly laughs along the way. How about you?

Exercise:

What can you do to lighten your life journey, experience more humor and laughter, and find a youthful, playful spirit that will bring more joy into your world?

#50: "When one door closes, another opens; but we often look so long and so regretfully upon the closed door that we do not see the one that has opened for us."

– Alexander Graham Bell, Scottish inventor

Life is filled with many endings and beginnings. It has many twists, turns, and even its share of dead ends. How can we maintain life's momentum when we come to a real or apparent ending?

It often takes us a while to turn our heads and look forward, to grasp the doorknob of the future and open it with excitement and enthusiasm.

Exercise:

What doors in your life have recently closed, and what new openings are available for you to pursue?

#51: "When at a conflict between mind and heart, always follow your heart."

– Swami Vivekananda, Indian Hindu monk

How do you make decisions? Do you make them with logic or do you check in with your gut? Do they make sense or do they feel right? Do you decide with your head or with your heart?

Many people use both, and enjoy knowing that something is consistent with their core values as well as meeting the criteria of logic and critical thinking.

What if these two types of thinking are in conflict? How often have you been faced with such a conflict in your personal or professional life, and how successful have you been in making such decisions?

Exercise:

Where could increasing your emphasis on following your heart increase your success and satisfaction?

#52: "Progress is impossible without change, and those who cannot change their minds cannot change anything."

– George Bernard Shaw, Irish playwright

I heard once that the reason many of us resist change is because we are afraid of losing something. It may be the fear of losing the familiar (better the devil you know), fear of losing control, or the fear of losing a relationship.

But what if we look at the flip side: the opportunities, the things we have to gain? Perhaps if we not only acknowledge that change is constant, but fully embrace it, even intentionally cause it, we can live fuller and more satisfying lives.

Exercise:

Where are you resisting change and maintaining a closed mind?

How can you develop a more open perspective to welcoming change in your world?

#53: "Do what you know is right, do the best you can, and let the loose ends drag."

– Unknown

Life is a journey. It's a game of progress, not perfection. When we live a life true to our nature and give it our all, perhaps we just need to let the chips fall where they may.

If we let go of the loose ends of life – the small stuff, the minor parts – then we can travel lighter.

Exercise:

Where do you sweat the small stuff, or major in the minors?

How can you simply let the loose ends drag?

#54: "The longest journey is the journey inward."

– Dag Hammarskjold, Swedish diplomat, economist and author

As I write this, I have just finished driving 845 miles over two days through Canada, New York, Vermont, and New Hampshire. My journey included stops in Niagara Falls, the Finger Lakes, a winery, and a very cool diner with the best all-you-can-eat fish and chips I've ever had!

Most people I know like going on such adventures. This quote, however, is about our ability to journey within our own minds. Think about it: you can instantly go anywhere at any time (and you don't even need to pay for gas).

Exercise:

Where have you already gone on this inner journey? What new and expanded adventures are possible for each day, week, month, and year ahead?

#55: "The work will wait while you show the child the rainbow, but the rainbow won't wait while you finish the work."

– Patricia Clifford (*attrib.*)

Are you missing too many rainbows? Do you sometimes feel that life is passing you by? Do you tell yourself that you will have the time in the future – perhaps during the weekend or on vacation, or even when you retire – to get to the things that matter?

We cannot schedule life's rainbows. We have to seize the precious moments when they occur.

Exercise:

How can you be more intentionally tuned into your world and find greater joy and fulfillment in life's special moments?

#56: "Life is playfulness. We need to play so that we can rediscover the magic all around us."

– Flora Colao (*attrib.*)

As a child, I remember being told, "You cannot go out and play until the work is done." It turned out that there was always work to do – in the form of chores and schoolwork.

Years ago, I took a one-year course called "The Wisdom Course" that was all about bringing greater playfulness into my life. It was around this time that I left my 12-year corporate job to begin my coaching career.

As the saying goes, "When you love what you do, you'll never work another day in your life." Most days, my work feels like play.

Exercise:

How can you bring greater magic into your life by bringing more playfulness into your work and your personal life?

#57: "If you go looking for a friend, you're going to find they're very scarce. If you go out to be a friend, you'll find them everywhere."

– Zig Ziglar, American motivational speaker

Among the many positive qualities exhibited by Zig Ziglar was his focus on giving, and being generous to others. In this quote, he suggests we give of ourselves through acts of sincere friendship – which in turn will encourage those around us to reciprocate.

The key is that we go first, instead of hoping that others will go first. There may be potential risk and the possibility of rejection – however, we know that without such risk, our lives will be a bit emptier.

Exercise:

Make the extra effort today to further extend your friendship efforts to those around you. Take note of the positive reactions you receive as a result of your sincere gestures.

#58: "Autumn is a second spring where every leaf is a flower."

– Albert Camus, French author and philosopher

Our society embraces youth, beauty, and vitality. These qualities seem to coincide with the spring and summer, where new growth begins and we bloom into our fullness.

As we age, we enter the autumn of our lives. I embrace this metaphor of leaves, in all their wondrous colors, being a second spring. With the life experience of age, we can discover new forms of inner beauty and wisdom.

Exercise:

How can you embrace every moment and every season of your life? What beauty can you find in where you are and who you have become?

#59: "Shoot for the moon. Even if you miss, you'll land among the stars."

– Unknown

Have you seen Westerns, military shows, or movies which included the phrase, "Ready, aim, fire"? Whether it is shooting at the moon or focusing on a critical goal, your desire to take each of these steps is necessary.

Some people and organizations suffer from the paralysis of analysis where the phrase might sound like, "Ready, aim ... aim ... aim ..."

The act of taking the shot or taking action allows us to see what happens when we miss the mark, and also allows us to adjust our aim to hit our target next time.

Exercise:

How can you take more shots today toward your intended target? Look for ways to learn what there is to learn when you miss – and also adjust your aim to hit the mark on your next attempt.

#60: "To raise new questions, new possibilities, to regard old problems from a new angle, requires creative imagination and marks real advance in science."

– Albert Einstein, German American theoretical physicist

When I was in school, success was all about getting the correct answer. In recent years, I have become fascinated by powerful questions and the fact that there are often many possible answers.

I am becoming far more comfortable with ambiguity and shades of gray. Einstein, through his study of quantum physics and his quotes pertaining to the mysteries life demonstrates, has helped lead me (and many others) in this direction.

Exercise:

How can you use powerful questions, your creativity, and your imagination to find the added strength and capacity to advance your life?

#61: "Whatever you vividly imagine, ardently desire, sincerely believe and enthusiastically act upon must inevitably come to pass."

– Paul J. Meyer, American personal development author and speaker

www.pauljmeyer.com

How many blogs, newsletters, and books have you seen that tout the "X steps to success" and then take a few hundred pages to describe them?

Meyer's quote contains four simple steps:

- **imagine** = dreams = vision
- **desire** = passion = purpose
- **believe** = core values = authenticity
- **act** = results = achievement

Exercise:

Select one area of your personal or professional life and go through these steps.

Repeat as often as you wish.

#62: "Don't ask yourself what the world needs; ask yourself what makes you come alive and then go and do that. Because what the world needs is people who have come alive."

– Howard Thurman, African American author and philosopher

I support a strength-based approach to work performance and life in general. The work of many individuals, including Marcus Buckingham, has established that the average person works in their area of strength perhaps only 20–25% of the time. However, some of the most satisfied and highly successful people work in their areas of strength and unique abilities 40–50% of the time.

Exercise:

How could you design your life and career to shoot for spending 60%, 70% or even 80% of your time working within your areas of strength?

If you did this, how alive would you be? What difference would you make in your life and the lives of those around you?

#63: "There are powers inside of you, which, if you could discover and use, would make of you everything you ever dreamed or imagined you could become."

– Orison Swett Marden, American self-help author

What are we capable of? What is our fullest potential as human beings? Perhaps we can consider the Guinness Book of World Records or the Olympics as a starting point.

We might think about great feats in areas such as:

- Speed at running, or swimming
- Endurance and strength
- Throwing, climbing, jumping, shooting...
- Writing and speaking
- Mathematics and sciences
- The arts, music, or other creative disciplines
- Memory (such as in a spelling bee)

Exercise:

With the above capacities already realized by human beings, what would a "world-record you" be capable of?

#64: "Be thankful for what you have; you'll end up having more. If you concentrate on what you don't have, you will never, ever have enough."

– Oprah Winfrey, American talk show host

I watched the final three episodes of Oprah's 25 years on television – and remembered how big an impact she has had on so many people. Her mantra has always been, "Live your best life." She always provided programming to help people do just that.

This quote, however, indicates the importance of accepting and being grateful for all of our blessings. It points to the current abundance in our worlds and in our lives, and shows how being thankful seems to attract even more good things.

Exercise:

Create a list of all the things in your life that you are thankful for, and keep asking yourself, "What else?"

I hope you get writer's cramp!

#65: "Life is a great big canvas, and you should throw all the paint you can on it."

– Danny Kaye, American performer

Many of us were given a box of crayons or set of watercolor paints as children. As we began drawing or painting, we often made a mess, and went beyond the workbook or the canvas. Our teachers and parents, with the best of intentions, taught us to paint by numbers and draw within the boundaries.

How does this idea relate to the lives that we live today: following the rules, sticking to established procedures, conforming?

Exercise:

What if you are simply a brilliant artist and your life is your masterpiece? How big a canvas, and how much paint, will you need? Consider doubling it.

#66: "Is the juice worth the squeezing?"

– Proverbial

When she was a child, my mother lived in an apartment above the fruit store her father owned. She would sometimes help him polish the apples and display the fruit as attractively as possible to attract customers.

Have you ever bitten into a shiny apple, only to find out that what was inside was mushy? You would never use such apples for juice.

Exercise:

Look at your own life as a fruit basket of people and experiences. Where are you putting your efforts? Is the juice of your life worth the squeezing?

#67: "Friendship is a soul dwelling in two bodies."

– Aristotle, classical Greek philosopher

In my first career, I was a science teacher. I have always been fascinated by what makes things work.

When we shift our perspective from the macro to the micro, the rules really get strange: consider the infinite universe and the infinitely small quantum world. I like the thought that there is some unifying force that holds everything together in some way.

I consider friendships and other close relationships as a place where we get to experience this special magical force. We can't see it, but when we have that deep soulful feeling, it is there.

Exercise:

Examine your very special relationships and their soulful quality and determine how you can take this experience to an even higher level.

#68: "If you do everything calmly, with intense concentration, you'll do everything at the correct speed."

– Paramahansa Yogananda, Indian yogi and guru

We all have an optimum rhythm or speed of life. If you play golf, what is your optimal club head speed? If you run, what is your optimal speed for a 5K? If you drive a car, what is your preferred speed for highway driving, to have you arrive safely?

Exercise:

What critical activities do you engage in each day? At what speed do you find your optimal effectiveness? Where do you need to develop greater calmness and concentration to find your correct speed of life?

#69: "Ah, but a man's reach should exceed his grasp, or what's a heaven for?"

– Robert Browning, English poet and playwright

In 1989, Robert Fritz wrote a book called *The Path of Least Resistance*. A key concept from this book is "Creative Tension." Fritz describes this special form of tension as an attractive force that pulls and draws us from our "current reality" to our "committed vision."

"I'm looking forward to the weekend" is a good example of positive creative tension. Many people, however, do not look forward to Mondays, due to their unfulfilling careers.

With this simple concept in mind, maybe all we need to do each day is to formulate something worth reaching for, beyond our current grasp.

Exercise:

What will you reach for today, tomorrow, and in the future? Perhaps you will even experience a bit more heaven, here on earth.

#70: "Love the giver more than the gift."

– Brigham Young, American head of the Mormon Church

I read *The Five Love Languages* many years ago, to enhance my relationship with my wife. I often recommend it to my coaching clients, to help them better understand their partners. The gist of the book is that we have different ways of showing love to one another. We almost always choose to show love in the same way that we like to receive it.

By tuning into one another's offerings of love, we can embrace these gifts in the way they are intended – instead of missing the message because we're simply not speaking the same love language.

Exercise:

How could you fully love the givers in your life by fully embracing every gift they have to offer, in their language?

#71: "Just do what you do best."

– Red Auerbach, American basketball coach

As parents, my wife and I were always focused on our children's growth and development. From the moment they were born, we often asked ourselves questions like, "What will they become?" and "How can we support their success?"

I believe that we, as parents, are caretakers of these young souls, for the purposes of both keeping them safe and secure, and exposing them to the world to discover their gifts and talents through the various experiences and opportunities through their life journey.

Exercise:

To what extent are you (and those closest to you) doing what you do best? What efforts can you make to further discover and express these unique abilities in the future?

#72: "A man's life is interesting primarily when he has failed – I well know. For it's a sign that he tried to surpass himself."

– Georges Clemenceau, French journalist, physician, and statesman

During the Olympics, each country, team, and individual is highly focused on winning gold. What does it mean to the individuals who do not make it to the Olympics, or who do not make it through the preliminaries, the semi-finals, or stand on the podium with a medal?

The 2012 Olympics had about 16,000 athletes for a world that contains over 7 billion people. How many medals were actually won and how many athletes, by the lack of a medal, "failed"?

Consider the much greater number of athletes who experience the powerful, often quiet, victory of achieving their personal best.

Exercise:

What would be needed in order for you to continually strive to surpass yourself?

What would be involved in achieving a "ten" in living? Or, to put it another way, what would you have to do to achieve a gold medal life?

#73: "Be always at war with your vices, at peace with your neighbors, and let each new year find you a better man."

– Benjamin Franklin, diplomat, inventor, and Founding Father of the United States

I like bargains and two-for-one sales. This quote is a three-for-one! In Ben Franklin's time, the word "vices" perhaps meant "behaviors that do not better oneself or another." Today, I suggest we consider the word "habits" instead.

The idea of being a better person points to our ability to learn, grow, and improve as individuals.

Exercise:

What habits or vices will you declare war upon? Which relationships in your life are ones where you will make a stand for peace? In what ways do you intend to be a better person next year, versus today?

#74: "Hardening of the heart ages people faster than hardening of the arteries."

– William James, psychologist and philosopher

Do you know anyone in your life who is a grumpy old man or woman? They don't even need to be chronologically old – they simply act old by:

- Looking for what's wrong in things and others
- Being skeptical and cynical
- Being overly serious
- Not smiling enough
- Not looking for the beauty around them

Exercise:

To clear out your arteries and find your own fountain of youth, try:

- Finding what's right and what works
- Being open and receptive to the thoughts and ideas of others
- Working on building your funny bone and your sense of humor
- Smiling and saying "thank you" more often
- Creating a daily gratitude and/or beauty journal to begin seeing the world with a lighter heart

#75: "Don't judge each day by the harvest you reap, but the seeds you plant."

– Robert Louis Stevenson, Scottish novelist and poet

Harvest time is only a small part of the growing season. My wife and I grew tomatoes last summer, and we sure enjoyed harvesting them at the end of August.

The process of growing them, though, was a bit more involved and time consuming. It included purchasing seeds, preparing the soil, watering, providing sunlight, adding plant food, watering, adding more plant food, more watering, you get the idea!

Exercise:

What seeds can you plant today? What care and attention will they need daily, so that you can have a successful harvest in the future?

Make sure you enjoy the process of gardening and not just the sweet fruits of life at harvest time.

#76: "The master in the art of living makes little distinction between his work and his play, his labor and his leisure, his mind and his body, his information and his recreation, his love and his religion. He hardly knows which is which. He simply pursues his vision of excellence at whatever he does, leaving others to decide whether he is working or playing. To him he's always doing both."

– James Michener, author

When I was a young boy, my dad used to tell me that I had to get all my work done before I could go out and play. At that time, work and play were definitely separated. One was hard and difficult; the other was fun and exciting.

When we see adults for whom this distinction does not exist, it helps us make a life-altering shift. Work and play can be one and the same.

Exercise:

How can you play at work and work at play?

What level of life satisfaction would be possible?

How can you be an inspiration to others to do the same?

#77: "Life's most persistent and urgent question is, 'What are you doing for others?'"

– Martin Luther King, Jr., American Civil Rights leader

Coaches love questions: digging for the answer provides great satisfaction. This one is a doozy. Martin Luther King, Jr., is considered by many one of the most inspirational leaders, and he spent his life with a dream. He put in a massive effort to serve others. He walked his talk.

Exercise:

What is your current answer to the question, "What are you doing for others?" What would you like your answer to be at the end of the day – and perhaps at the end of your days?

#78: "To finish the moment, to find the journey's end in every step of the road, to live the greatest number of good hours, is wisdom."

– Ralph Waldo Emerson, American essayist

What does it mean to live a good hour? It could mean:

- Being fully present to each person and fully engaged in each experience

- Living in the moment, not dwelling on the past or daydreaming solely of the future

- Living a life of meaning and purpose beyond your own concerns

- Being generous and sharing your special gifts and resources with others

- Learning and growing in some way each day, and sharing your knowledge and life experiences with others

Exercise:

What does living a good hour include for you?

What next step will you take to move toward greater wisdom?

#79: "Creativity involves breaking out of established patterns in order to look at things in a different way."

– Edward de Bono, doctor and author

www.edwdebono.com

Years ago, I read *A Whole New Mind,* by Daniel Pink. The premise of this book was based on the importance and value of right-brain/non-linear thinking. Pink pointed to some of the critical limiting factors related to left-brain or linear thinking: the value of this type of thinking has decreased due to the advent of technology.

Exercise:

How much of your day do you spend on right-brain versus left-brain activities?

How can you break some of your established patterns and look at your world differently, to develop your creative mind?

#80: "No one who rises before dawn 360 days a year fails to make his family rich."

– Chinese proverb

When I was little, I remember waking up very early on Saturday mornings to watch cartoons. There were no VCRs or DVRs: if you didn't get up, you missed it!

As adults, many people begrudgingly wake up to go to work, in order to earn a living and take care of their families.

Exercise:

What would get you to leap out of bed each morning, with that excitement of youth? What skills could you master and what riches would you attract into your life?

How can you go beyond simply making a living to creating a richer and more fulfilling life?

#81: "The bad news is time flies. The good news is you're the pilot."

– Michael Altshuler, American motivational speaker

I recently attended a coaching conference where a speaker, Jim Selman, shared his work on the topic of aging. I was surprised to see just how significant and universal the subject was for the majority of conference participants – including myself.

What does it mean to age well? Why do many of us pursue the fountain of youth, through everything from plastic surgery to the next wonder drug?

How can we transform our views on aging, to impact our lives in the areas of health, happiness, self-expression, meaningful relationships, and the overall desire for purpose?

Exercise:

How will you pilot your life, given your answer to the question above, to make the most of the precious time that you have?

#82: "The ultimate test of a man's conscience may be his willingness to sacrifice something today for future generations whose words of thanks will not be heard."

– Gaylord Nelson, American Democrat

I once saw a behavioral experiment, conducted with small children of three or four years old. The experiment involved marshmallows. The child could have a single marshmallow immediately, or they could wait five minutes longer and be rewarded with two marshmallows.

Some of the children simply gobbled the one immediately. However, the children who were able to delay their gratification seemed far happier with their accomplishment.

Exercise:

What sacrifices are you willing to make today to help yourself and others have a far better future (even if you may never receive thanks or the rewards directly)?

What would you like your legacy to be?

#83: "There is nothing either good or bad, but thinking makes it so."

– William Shakespeare, English playwright

Our ability as humans to interpret the world around us is remarkable. Consider your thoughts about the following pairs of words:

- life – death
- win – lose
- happy – sad
- right – wrong
- power – force
- full – empty
- leadership – management
- optimism – pessimism
- young – old
- growth – decline
- success – failure
- strong – weak
- natural – artificial

Exercise:

Is there a fundamental "goodness" or "badness" in anything? How does your thinking about the world and others help you or limit you? How could you expand or shift your thinking to lead a far more fulfilling life?

#84: "Life is about not knowing, having to change, taking the moment and making the best of it without knowing what's going to happen next. Delicious ambiguity."

– Gilda Radner, American actress

I never knew Gilda Radner in any other way than in her comedic role on Saturday Night Live. I do remember how devastated Gene Wilder, her husband, was upon her passing.

There is now a wonderful organization, Gilda's Club, named after her. It aims to help individuals and their families make the most of the challenges of cancer and similar diseases.

Perhaps her life was a form of improv when she took each moment and each situation and made the best of it. After her death, people were inspired to make the best of even that situation – by setting up Gilda's Club.

Exercise:

How can you play and dance with the ambiguities of life and make more of your moments delicious?

#85: "In everyone's life, at some time, our inner fire goes out. It is then burst into flame by an encounter with another human being. We should all be thankful for those people who rekindle the inner spirit."

– Albert Schweitzer, German theologian

Have you ever noticed how life has lots of ups and downs? We experience the glories of victory and the agonies of defeat.

We have all heard the phrase, "This too shall pass." We eventually find our footing from our low points – and are brought down to earth from the peaks of life's mountains.

This quote is about the special people in our lives that bring out our very best and ignite the fullest possibilities of living.

Exercise:

Who are the advisors, mentors, coaches, family members and friends that provide you with this spark?

Have you thanked them lately?

Where could you help rekindle the fires of others?

#86: "It has been my observation that people are just about as happy as they make up their minds to be."

– Abraham Lincoln, 16th American President

Could it be that simple? Can we just make the choice to be happy?

We have all heard stories of people with great beauty, talent, and financial wealth who are miserable. We are also aware of entire societies where people have very limited worldly possessions, yet live joyful lives.

What's the secret? Can we actually be the architects of our own happy lives?

Abraham Lincoln refers to the word "mind" as the source. Today, there's the entire field of positive psychology to explore this in great detail.

Exercise:

Consider purchasing a copy of Martin Seligman's book *Authentic Happiness* or Tal Ben-Shahar's book *Happier,* and make up your own mind.

#87: "The way of a fool is right in his own eyes, but a wise man is he who listens to counsel."

– Proverbs 12:15, The Bible

Have you ever had someone say, "I know" when you share something with them? Doesn't that just drive you crazy? Or, worse, how often do others interrupt you to fill in the remainder of what they were expecting you to say?

Both of these situations indicate that others are not listening – or that they're simply far more interested in their own favorite subject: themselves.

When we fully listen to others and truly consider their ideas, we expand our world view beyond our individual perspectives. "A mind, once expanded, never fully shrinks back to its original state."

Exercise:

Where in your life can you develop greater wisdom, by listening more fully to others? Remember, "You have two ears and one mouth – use them proportionally."

#88: "Friendships multiply joys and divide grief."

– Henry George Bohn, British publisher

There is a good reason why we are social creatures. We simply live and survive better when we are part of a community. Our friendships tend to be very intentional in their ability to move us forward in life.

Have you ever noticed that successes are far sweeter when celebrated with friends and family? How much better do you feel when you experience sadness, disappointment, and grief in the company of others, versus going it alone?

Exercise:

Which friends multiple your joy and divide your grief? How can you show them your gratitude?

Who in your life today would benefit from your special friendship?

#89: "Death is Nature's expert advice to get plenty of Life."

– Goethe, German writer

We have all received the advice to get plenty of rest, exercise, water, quality food, fresh air, etc. I love the idea of getting plenty of life.

We could also think about having more:

- love
- laughter
- adventure
- beauty
- quality
- risk
- excitement
- learning

Exercise:

Select 5 – 15 actions that you will take to help you get plenty of life.

If you want extra credit, try thinking of at least one action for each letter of the alphabet. Share this list with others.

#90: "Discontent is the first step in the progress of a man or nation."

– Oscar Wilde, Irish writer and poet

This quote seems a bit contrary to the idea of being happy with who you are and what you have, and living in the present. It does, however, point to a significant driving force for most of us – namely, the desire for growth and progress.

Exercise:

Where in your professional and personal life do you experience dissatisfaction or discontent? Which of these areas can be influenced and improved through your efforts?

Select one or two of these and make the needed changes to realize the progress you desire.

Find a coach or an accountability partner to help increase your chances of success.

#91: "That man is the richest whose pleasures are the cheapest."

– Henry D. Thoreau, American author and transcendentalist

My father Marvin, at the age of 87, is one of the people I most admire. He has always referred to himself as one of the richest men in the world. We lived very modestly in a row house in Philadelphia, and I can never recall him complaining about his life.

He includes among his past and present riches:

- A loving marriage
- A job as a teacher, coach and counselor, where he got to make a difference
- A happy family life with three wonderful kids (including me!)
- Good health
- Close and loyal friends
- A good sense of humor to laugh at life and even at himself

Exercise:

What are your personal riches that cost you little, yet bring you great wealth?

#92: "When love and skill work together, expect a masterpiece."

– John Ruskin, English artist and art critic

We have all heard the quote, "When you love what you do, you'll never work a day in your life." A by-product of this mixture of love and work is mastery, due to the amount of practice we experience over time.

Think about famous artists, top athletes, and great entertainers as examples of this synergistic combination.

Exercise:

What are your greatest skills, where you lose yourself in love? It would be wonderful if these included your vocation. They may be hobbies or similar avocations – and hopefully, they can include building extraordinary relationships, in all areas of life.

What masterpieces have you built to this point and what future works of art are on the way?

#93: "Rules and models destroy genius and art."

– William Hazlitt, English writer

Many historic thinkers have explored left-brain versus right-brain thinking. Modern-day thinkers often refer to the concept of linear or analytical thinking versus quantum or non-linear thought.

Whatever you call the two types, they are both highly useful and have their place in making the world work. As a business coach, I see many great examples where procedures and systems increase profits. Six Sigma, Kaizen, and other quality initiatives are widely used in organizations today.

Yet, when we overuse procedures to manage the abilities of people, we often diminish their ability to act, think, and create.

Exercise:

Where do rules in your professional and personal life serve you well, and where do they limit your creativity and genius?

How will you find the right balance?

#94: "Make happy those who are near and those who are far will come."

– Chinese proverb

Many years ago, I read a little book called *Fish,* which presented a simple set of concepts to improve every work environment. The concept I remember most is, "Make their day."

I get great pleasure looking for opportunities to add just a little bit more sunshine, one more smile, or an additional laugh to someone's day. (Pretty corny, huh?)

The people in this world who focus on others tend to attract more people and more opportunities into their lives. We speak about their personalities with terms like "charisma" and "magnetic."

Exercise:

What efforts do you take daily to support the happiness of others?

Who are the people in your life that bring you the greatest happiness?

What else can you do today and in the future to "make their day" and, in turn, attract more good things into your life?

#95: "There is a giant asleep within everyone. When that giant awakens, miracles happen."

– Frederick Faust, American author

Is the giant within you fully asleep, taking a catnap, or just a bit drowsy these days? What are some strategies to waken this giant to the status of full alert?

Exercise:

Consider the following ideas:

1. Identify the giants and leaders in your organization or community and practice similar behaviors.

2. Double your efforts on any worthwhile endeavor – and see what level of accomplishment results.

3. Cut the amount of time you give yourself to accomplish key tasks in half, to create greater urgency – and see what happens.

#96: "Often the greatest enemy of present happiness is past happiness too well remembered."

– Oscar Hammling, writer

Many of us long for the good old days, the years of our youth – where things seemed simpler and the stresses of the modern world didn't knock on our door, call us on our phone, or enter our email inboxes.

We selectively go into our memory banks and replay all those family vacations, personal adventures, and winning moments ... without any of the commercials that were there all along.

Exercise:

Consider the Kodak experience at Disney World. Perhaps "making memories" is what our days are for. With this perspective in mind, how do you intend to live this day?

#97: "Mishaps are like knives, that either serve us or cut us, as we grasp them by the blade or the handle."

– Herman Melville, American author

The word "mishap" seems a bit more open to interpretation than other words such as mistakes, errors, and failure. Whichever word you currently use to identify life's bumps in the road, it is our human ability to interpret these events that makes all the difference.

When we grab the blade of these events, we are stopped, defeated, or overcome. We tend to stay down and never do or try that again.

When we grab the handle, though, we see these events as opportunities to learn from, and improve our life and the world.

Exercise:

What mishaps have occurred recently in your life? How can you grab the handle, so the lessons you've learned will serve you in the future?

#98: "There are no shortcuts to anyplace worth going."

– Beverly Sills, American opera singer

I tend to believe in the quote by Gary Player, "The harder you work, the luckier you get."

Look at how we celebrate the great achievements of individuals and groups in sports and business: these people have put in the work to reach places worth going. How do you get to Carnegie Hall? Practice, practice, practice.

Exercise:

Where do you intend to go in this world that will make the journey worth all the effort?

What will be your long and winding road to success that will be worth the trip?

#99: "Don't be afraid to go out on a limb. That's where the fruit is."

– Unknown

Have you ever picked an apple from the trunk of a tree? Me neither! The sweetness of life can only be found when we go out on those proverbial limbs and take a risk.

We must face failure, change, getting hurt, and looking foolish in order to explore our visions and reach beyond our grasp. How else can we experience all that life has to offer?

Exercise:

Where are you playing it too safe, and missing out on the sweet fruits of life?

What are the limbs of life that you can climb out on, to reach what you deeply desire?

#100: "Even if you're on the right track, you'll get run over if you just sit there."

– Mark Twain, American author and humorist

This quote reminds me of one about climbing the ladders of life: we must be sure that the ladder is leaning against the correct wall.

As true as this may be, we must also be vigilant, placing one foot in front of the other to progress to our goals.

In my many years of coaching, I have seen some people continually set the same goals and objectives, putting in only modest effort and making minimal progress. In our rapidly moving world, an individual or organization that makes little or no progress often gets left behind by their competition.

Exercise:

What booster rockets, high-test fuel and massive action would it take for you to reach your goals faster and amaze yourself?

#101: "One's mind, once stretched by a new idea, never regains its original dimensions."

– Oliver Wendell Holmes, Sr., American doctor and writer

Yesterday, I went to a barbeque with friends and family. My father attended, as did a little three-and-a-half year old boy named Luka. Luka got my dad and others to play baseball with him.

I actually got to see Luka's understanding and abilities expand over the hours – resulting in significant pleasure and joy for everyone there.

Exercise:

How have you embraced the pleasure and joy of learning for yourself, and expanded your world?

What ideas do you have to share with others, to expand their worlds too?

#102: "The difference between ordinary and extraordinary is the little extra."

– Jimmy Johnson, football coach and broadcaster

Many years ago, I read a book called *The Slight Edge*, with the fundamental premise that doing that little bit extra makes a big difference in life.

In golf, it can be one stroke over the course of a four day tournament that wins the match. When running, it can be a single step or fraction of a second that makes the difference. And in horse racing, we have all heard the phrase, "Winning by a nose."

Exercise:

Where in your professional and personal life can you put forth that extra effort, to exceed the ordinary and to realize the extraordinary?

Choose this area now and tell someone close to you, so that you will receive that extra support you may need.

#103: "Success is a journey, not a destination."

– Arthur Ashe, American tennis player

To reach the end of our lives, at the very least, is to leave our physical world and perhaps enter a new level of existence. To some, the end of our lives is a more definitive end: death, with nothing beyond.

Life is one game I am not in a big hurry to finish. Taking pleasure in each step of this journey seems like a very good strategy.

How many people do you know who wish their lives away, by skipping steps in their journeys, by looking forward to the end of the work week, the end of the school year, or the opportunity to retire from a dead-end job?

Exercise:

How can you either change the game of your life, or shift your perspective, to make the most of each moment?

#104: "Teamwork is the ability to work together toward a common vision. The ability to direct individual accomplishment toward organizational objectives. It is the fuel that allows common people to attain uncommon results."

– Andrew Carnegie, Scottish-American industrialist

Let's face it: when it comes down to it, we're all a bit selfish. Who hasn't had the thought, "What's in it for me?" from time to time? People rarely will do something solely for the boss if there's little or no personal pay off.

It seems that all truly great teams understand this, and add this special factor of shared accomplishment to their own individual success. Even the acronym TEAM has been described as "Together, Everyone Achieves More."

Exercise:

How can you tap into both the individual and collective motives of your personal and professional communities to obtain the uncommon results you desire?

#105: "The only limit to our realization of tomorrow will be our doubts of today."

– Franklin D. Roosevelt, 32nd American President

When I work with my coaching clients, we always do various forms of questionnaires, and include their perspectives on the obstacles they face on their journey to personal success.

A number of personal character traits and habits often get revealed during these discussions. It's clear that the most limiting, destructive belief of all is self-doubt: fear prevents us from making the effort in the first place.

A common question coaches ask is, "If you knew you could not fail, what could you accomplish with your life?" We then follow this by asking, "What else?" a number of times, to help people explore the potential cost of this self-doubt.

Exercise:

How can you summon the courage to experience self-doubt and yet still take the actions needed to realize your brighter tomorrows?

#106: "Happiness is not a state to arrive at, but a manner of traveling."

– Samuel Johnson, English author, literary critic and lexicographer

I truly enjoy some of the deep and probing discussions I have with my clients as they explore their own success journeys.

One simple and useful discussion relating to happiness involves these three words: *be, do, have.*

People often get this process backwards. They believe that when they **have** "X", they will **do** "Y", and **be** happier.

As a coach, I encourage them to begin with their state of **being**, that informs their **doing**, that in turn will help them **have** the life they desire.

Exercise:

Revisit your list of core values and fundamental beliefs from the exercise for Quote #27, to find the source of your being, so you can be happier. What do you need to *do* to be happier?

#107: "The environment you fashion out of your thoughts, your beliefs, your ideals, your philosophy is the only climate you will ever live in."

– Stephen Covey, American self-help author

What if we could control the weather? What if we could live in our own inner San Diego all the time?

We have all heard the phrase that so-and-so has a "sunny disposition," or that they are shrouded in a "dark and stormy cloud."

Exercise:

How can you change your thoughts, beliefs and ideals, and live in a climate of your own creation?

How will doing so make each and every day a bit brighter?

For extra credit, share this ability with others, so that they too can fashion out their own more pleasant environments.

#108: "Most great men and women are not perfectly rounded in their personalities, but are instead people whose one driving enthusiasm is so great it makes their faults seem insignificant."

– Charles A. Cerami, American author

Many years ago, I read an article in a magazine entitled, "Life Balance is Bunk!"

When I work with clients, many indicate that living a balanced life is one of their primary objectives. But, if you study the world of personal and professional high achievement, you'll find two things.

First, high achievers lead very imbalanced lives. Second, they are very happy and have actually chosen this imbalance at this point in their lives.

Exercise:

Rebalance your life by adding more of some things and reducing – or even stopping – certain other activities. If you do this exercise often, you too will have a somewhat unbalanced but happier life.

#109: "Things turn out the best for the people who make the best of the way things turn out."

– John Wooden, American basketball coach

John Wooden is considered by many one of the most successful college-level coaches of all time. His record of championships and the number of superstar players coached by him are legendary.

Two of the primary gifts he gave his players were his great attitude and his work ethic. He always focused himself and his players on making the most of each situation – resulting in exemplary individual and team performances.

Exercise:

To what degree do you make the best of the way things turn out?

What adjustments can you make to your behavior and attitude, in order to win your own championships?

#110: "Character is like a tree and reputation like its shadow. The shadow is what we think of it; the tree is the real thing."

– Abraham Lincoln, 16th American President

Who are you and how do you behave when no one is watching? Are your values expressed in your deeds at all times – or only when you are on display for others to see?

Golf is a sport of great character, where the participants actually call penalties on themselves – even when their playing partners rarely, if ever, see these penalties.

Exercise:

What are your daily standards for living a life of honor and integrity? To what values do you hold true, so that you always live in this manner, regardless of whether an audience is there to observe?

What changes will you make to focus on the tree (character), rather than its shadow (reputation)?

#111: "Quality is never an accident; it is always the result of high intention, sincere effort, intelligent direction, and skillful execution; it represents the wise choice of many alternatives."

– William A. Foster, American Marine *(attrib.)*

Six Sigma, TQM, and Lean Manufacturing are processes that many organizations use to build quality into their products and services. These programs, when successfully implemented, meet all the attributes of high intentionality, sincere effort, intelligent direction, and skillful execution.

Exercise:

How can you apply these characteristics to build strong relationships, a rewarding career, and an outstanding life?

What wise choices will you make today and into the future to do just that?

#112: "To dream anything that you want to dream. That is the beauty of the human mind. To do anything that you want to do. That is the strength of the human will. To trust yourself, to test your limits. That is the courage to succeed."

– Bernard Edmonds, writer

How often do you test your limits?

How often do you bump up against your comfort zone and stop right there in relative safety?

Is there a secret to realizing our dreams? Archimedes said that if you had a long enough lever, you could move the world.

I'd like you to consider the idea that your commitments are your levers. By using your mind to envision a better future, and then by mobilizing your strength and courage, you can move beyond your self-imposed limits.

Exercise:

List three to five of your highest-priority commitments that are essential for you to consider your life a success.

What can you do today to fulfill these commitments and exceed your limits?

#113: "Well done is better than well said."

– Benjamin Franklin, diplomat, inventor, and Founding Father of the United States

Do you walk your talk? Based on this quote, Ben Franklin must have spent some time in Missouri, the "show-me" state.

We have all heard the phrase that "talk is cheap" and we all know that thoughts only become things when acted upon.

Exercise:

Get out three or four brightly colored Post-it® notes and write the following on each of them: *What is the most important thing to do now?*

Place these Post-it® notes in strategic places in your world, to increase your propensity for action.

#114: "It's what you learn after you know it all, that counts."

– John Wooden, American basketball coach

When you hear a person say, "I know," it means that they have stopped listening. When a cup is full, it is impossible to fill it any further.

Consider the possibility that knowledge and wisdom are vital fluids that fill your life's cup. What if the richness of life could only be held in your cupped hands? What a waste to limit yourself in this way.

Exercise:

How can you dramatically increase the size of your learning vessel, to allow greater knowledge and wisdom in?

How can you, as a scholar of life, have a beginner's mind, and make the new things you learn count even more?

#115: "Our chief want in life is somebody who will make us do what we can."

– Ralph Waldo Emerson, American essayist

When I begin a coaching assignment, I include a core value exercise. Often, my clients include the values of personal growth and realizing their potential on their list.

My own journey into the world of coaching began when I watched the 1992 Barcelona Olympic Games, where there were approximately 2,000 coaches supporting 5,000 athletes. It seemed that Olympic levels of achievement were highly correlated with the support of a coach to help each individual achieve their best performance.

Exercise:

What percent of your fullest potential have you realized, professionally and personally?

Who are the people in your life that encourage and stretch you to be and do all you can?

#116: "A great pleasure in life is doing what people say you cannot do."

– Walter Bagehot, English businessman and essayist

In your day to day life, notice how often you see people being critical or diminishing others with phrases such as:

- That will never work.
- You can't do that.
- Why bother trying?
- It's too difficult.

How often do statements such as these stop you in your tracks? Perhaps instead, as is the case with this quote, they generate thoughts like:

- Oh yeah?
- Yes, I can.
- I'll show you.
- Your thinking just makes me want it more.

Exercise:

Where are your colleagues at work, family members, and even people who you call friends placing their limiting beliefs on you?

Explore what it will take to exceed these limits, achieve your objectives, and tell yourself, "I knew I had it in me all along!"

#117: "The quality of a person's life is in direct proportion to their commitment to excellence, regardless of their chosen field of endeavor."

– Vince Lombardi, American football coach

I have had the honor of coaching over 1,000 individuals over 21 years.

Among their common characteristics was the pursuit of excellence in all areas of their lives. I even named my six-month coaching program "Personal Excellence Training", where each person gets to plan and execute their own personal excellence journey.

You can find out more about that program here:

www.dempcoaching.com/personal-excellence-training

Exercise:

List five to ten of the most important areas of your life.

The list may include family, career, health, finances, community, faith, relationships, education, service, leadership, sports, skills, hobbies, travel, etc.

Answer the following question for each area you listed: *What would I be able to accomplish if I fully pursued personal excellence in the area of family (career, health, etc.)?*

#118: "People seldom improve when they have no other model but themselves to copy after."

– Oliver Goldsmith, Irish writer

When I was a young boy, I loved to play tennis. Although short in stature, I was very quick on my feet, and would often out-hustle, and out-last, my playing opponents. I was actually pretty good!

One day, I noticed that I was no longer doing so much running around and actually had opponents on the run, due to the well-placed shots I was able to hit.

I continued to play with the same people, and found myself winning almost every match. The downside of this was that my skills plateaued, or actually declined a bit, due to the lack of skilled opponents.

In today's tennis world, I would simply be moved from a 3.5 level to a 4.0 level and my growth would likely begin again.

Exercise:

Where in your life have you reached the top ranks of performance and plateaued in your growth?

Where can you find others with superior skills and ability to help you stretch your limits and take your growth to the next level?

#119: "Far better it is to dare mighty things, to win glorious triumphs, even though checkered by failure, than to take rank with those poor spirits who neither enjoy much nor suffer much, because they live in the gray twilight that knows not victory nor defeat."

– Theodore Roosevelt, 26th American President

How often do you find yourself on the playing field versus in the stands as a spectator?

As spectators to a sporting event, or even a business interaction, we find ourselves in a relatively safe spot where we risk little or nothing. When we actually suit up and get in the game, we are putting ourselves to the test. Will we win and achieve success, or will we lose and fail?

One sure thing is that without risk, without getting in the game, we will never truly test ourselves, grow fully, and turn our potential for success into glorious triumphs.

Exercise:

Where in your life and career can you shift from being a spectator to getting on the field, so as to experience the excitement of participating and potential victory – and yes, the possibility of defeat?

#120: "Genius does take shortcuts, but it rarely escapes initial drudgery."

– William Feather, American publisher and author *(attrib.)*

Have you ever noticed a person with great mastery or skill who accomplishes feats of brilliance with ease?

Whether that's an inventor like Edison, an athlete like Michael Jordan, or performers like the Beatles, they all have something in common. They all experience the not so glowing moments of poor performance, drudgery, or failure.

The eventual moments of success so often come after massive amounts of preparation, without the accolades and standing ovations that we see in the media.

Exercise:

Where does your genius lie, beneath your seemingly mundane daily efforts?

How can you take delight in these efforts, knowing that there's a great gift just waiting to be revealed?

#121: "Adversity reveals genius, prosperity conceals it."

– Horace, Roman poet

I remember, in my mid-30's, talking with some colleagues about our 401k program at work. The company had just developed an easy-to-use software program that helped people calculate their net worth based on their savings level, years of work, and a hypothetical interest rate estimate.

My colleagues' goal was to retire, to stop working, to take it easy, to relax. By increasing their prosperity, though, they seemed to diminish their drive.

On the other hand, I've seen people who've experienced great adversity and very limited resources tap into their inner abilities and courage to accomplish great things no one would ever expect.

Exercise:

Assuming you achieve your desired level of prosperity, how will you keep your passion and drive each and every day to fully realize your genius?

#122: "Of all knowledge, the wise and good seek most to know themselves."

– William Shakespeare, English playwright

The pursuit of knowledge is a never-ending journey. Whether we wish to win the national spelling bee or master our own vocation, the inner journey to amass the necessary amount of information is daunting.

The journey within oneself can be mysterious and enlightening. After all, wherever you go, there you are.

Commit to a personal journey of inner discovery and self-awareness. Discover your strengths. If you are not sure what they are, ask those close to you. Discover your unique abilities and talents. Discover your core values and fundamental beliefs.

Exercise:

Consider creating a daily self-discovery journal or log to capture your observations. Share those observations with a close colleague or family member.

#123: "There is no medicine like hope, no incentive so great and no tonic so powerful as expectation of something better tomorrow."

– Orison Swett Marden, American self-help author

We all have them: good days, and not so good days. If you would like to increase the number of good ones, work on your optimism muscle, always hoping for (and, yes, working toward) a better future.

Consider the difference between the hopeful worker on a Friday, looking forward to the weekend, versus the sad and blue individual on a Sunday evening, not so delighted about the Monday ahead.

Exercise:

Ask yourself these questions, whether you are in a good mood or not, to provide yourself and others with a tonic for a better tomorrow:

- What am I looking forward to?

- What can I work on today, to make my tomorrow better?

- How can I be a catalyst for others to have their tomorrows be great too?

#124: "The real voyage of discovery consists not in seeking new landscapes, but in having new eyes."

– Marcel Proust, French novelist

Imagine seeing life through the following pairs of eyes:

- The eyes of an infant
- The eyes of a toddler
- The eyes of a fifth-grader
- The eyes of a teenager
- The eyes of a young adult
- The eyes of a Generation-X-er
- The eyes of a baby boomer
- The eyes of a senior citizen
- The eyes of a person of the opposite sex
- The eyes of a person of a different religion or background
- The eyes of a person of a different race
- The eyes of a more analytic, or more creative, person

... you get the idea!

Exercise:

What expanded value do you discover when shifting your perspective? How can you continue to look at the world through many sets of eyes in the future, to expand and enhance your life?

#125: "Life is no straight and easy corridor along which we travel free and unhampered, but a maze of passages, through which we must seek our way, lost and confused, now and again checked in a blind alley. But always, if we have faith, a door will open for us, not perhaps one that we ourselves would ever have thought of, but one that will ultimately prove good for us."

– A.J. Cronin, Scottish physician and novelist

How did you get where you are today? How many twists and turns, roadblocks, forks in the road, and dead-ends have you found on your journey? The shortest distance between two points may be a straight line – however, life virtually never works out this way.

We often get upset when our intentions are thwarted and our expectations are unfulfilled, in spite of our knowledge of how life works. Perhaps our job is simply to look within ourselves in faith, and take the first step.

Exercise:

How has following your internal GPS helped you make some of your life choices?

During those points of decision, how were you able to turn a dead end into an open door?

#126: "A friend is a loved one who awakens your life in order to free the wild possibilities within you."

– John O'Donohue, Irish poet, philosopher and priest

Someone once told me that friends are the family we choose for ourselves. That puts friendships in a very special category of relationships.

One of the key attributes of our friends is that they are tuned into our personal life frequencies. We are far better together than apart.

Exercise:

What are two to three areas of your life that need to be awakened? What would you consider to be a wild possibility in these areas?

Who are the friends that bring this special spark to your life – and how can you be this kind of friend for others?

#127: "Ultimately the measure of every human being is their capacity to awaken the love in themselves and to extend it to their fellow man."

– Mick Brown, English journalist and author *(paraphrasing Bede Griffiths)*

www.twitter.com/mickbrownwriter

As a business and personal coach, I deal with many practical and quantifiable issues facing my clients. Beneath the surface of these objective details are the softer sides of things.

The term "love" is often considered off-limits in business – yet I find that it is frequently the hidden foundation of outstanding results. There is great power and connectivity that brings great possibilities to life, when we awaken and extend love to those around us.

A smile, a caring ear, a helpful act of service, a thank-you, and even a hug from time to time are some simple things we can do.

Exercise:

What are some other ways you can extend your loving nature to others?

#128: "Our greatest glory consists not in never falling, but in rising every time we fall."

– Ralph Waldo Emerson, American essayist

One of my favorite movies of all time is *Rudy,* where the main character is a small and very feisty football player with a passion for the University of Notre Dame.

Through dogged determination, persistence, and a tenacity rarely seen, he takes quite a beating by being a veritable practice dummy for the first team – and eventually rises to glory in the final hours.

Exercise:

What are your passions, commitments, and strivings where you continue to give it your all – no matter how often you fall?

What inspiring "Rudy" stories have you observed, and participated in?

What stories are yet to be written, where you will experience future glorious moments?

#129: "Become so wrapped up in something that you forget to be afraid."

– Lady Bird Johnson, American First Lady

My journey into the coaching profession is definitely an example of getting so wrapped up in something I almost forgot to be afraid.

At the ripe old age of 35, I threw caution to the wind and left a 12-year career with a Fortune 500 pharmaceutical company to sign up for the job of "coach" with:

1. No salary (you ate what you killed!)

2. No benefits

3. No coaching clients

4. No general agreement about or awareness of the profession (it was truly in its infancy)

5. A wife and two young children (plus a considerable mortgage)

6. Modest savings (with about 6 months of living expenses)

In spite of these factors, I found myself very enthusiastic and excited to partner with people and help them achieve breakthroughs in their personal and professional lives – just as Olympic athletes work with coaches to achieve their full potential.

Exercise:

Where can you be so wrapped up in something that you forget to be afraid?

#130: "Act so as to elicit the best in others and thereby in thyself."

– Felix Adler, German professor of political and social ethics

This quote is perhaps one of the closest to the core message of coaching: "Bring out the best in others." Most people have an inherent desire to be their very best and to realize their fullest potential.

Many of our schools, our religious institutions, even our families, utilize an "outside-in" training method for development. This approach fosters conformity, and often limits creative self-expression.

Coaches believe that many answers and capacities already lie within us. When others elicit these answers and capacities, the growth we experience is both more enjoyable and sustainable.

Exercise:

Who are the people in your life that elicit the best from you?

Where can you be a coach and elicit the best from others?

#131: "In the face of uncertainty, there is nothing wrong with hope."

– Bernie Siegel, MD, American author, pediatric and general surgeon

www.berniesiegelmd.com

Many people would agree that we live in uncertain times. Consider the economy, politics, terrorism, new technology, and globalization as examples of dramatic and rapid change, both positive and negative.

We humans are the reasons for such change ... yet, we also have a solid, unchanging, foundation of faith, security, resilience, and hope for a brighter future.

This hope is like a beacon of light from a lighthouse on a stormy day, showing us the way into a safe harbor.

Exercise:

How can you further develop and fully express your most hopeful spirit in today's uncertain world?

#132: "The human spirit is stronger than anything that can happen to it."

– George C. Scott, American actor, director and producer

What does the human spirit mean to you? Consider the following:

- The capacity to achieve great and wondrous things
- The ability to learn and apply what you learn
- The capacity to forgive
- The ability to love and be loved
- The capacity to be creative and innovative
- The ability to dream and envision a better future
- The capacity to endure pain and life's difficult or even tragic moments
- The ability to be resilient and try again and again in spite of repeated failures or defeats

Exercise:

Who are some of the people you know who demonstrate a strong human spirit?

What qualities do they demonstrate that you admire and wish to emulate?

#133: "There are some people who live in a dream world, and there are some who face reality; and then there are those who turn one into the other."

– Douglas Everett *(attrib.)*

This quote sums up a primary reason why I am a coach. It may have been the reason I was inspired by the 1992 Olympic Games to pursue a coaching career.

The fundamental idea of turning one's dreams into reality puts a smile on my face whenever I see the realization of this through the individual and collective efforts of my clients.

Two books related to this subject by Wayne Dyer are: *The Power of Intention* and *Manifest Your Destiny*. What will your dreams include as you envision a gold medal life?

Exercise:

Consider reading Dyer's books and some other recommended books from my website to further realize your dreams:

www.dempcoaching.com/recommended-reading

#134: "The winds and waves are always on the side of the ablest navigators."

– Edward Gibbon (*attrib.*)

Although we all know that it is impossible to control the wind and the waves of life, I do like the concept that as we travel life's journey, we can still be capable navigators.

Exercise:

What adjustments can you make to your life's rudders and sails to pursue your personal and professional goals, in spite of rough seas and strong headwinds?

#135: "Behind every able man, there are always other able men."

– Chinese Proverb

Whenever you read the acknowledgements section of a book, observe an acceptance speech, or observe someone who looks back on a life well lived, one thing is clear: no one accomplishes anything great alone.

Who are the family members, mentors, colleagues, coaches, advisors, etc., who have assisted you along the way?

Exercise:

How clear are these people about the difference they have made in your life? Which of these people might you want to acknowledge today?

Of these people, who would put you on their list?

#136: "I know of no more encouraging fact than the unquestionable ability of man to elevate his life by conscious endeavor."

– Henry David Thoreau, American author and philosopher

One of the most satisfying things about being a coach is that I get to watch and participate in people's conscious efforts to improve their lives. I get to ask them deep, probing questions about where they wish to move forward – and I get to watch them courageously turning these insights into action.

Unfortunately, some people don't have adequate support to bring these unconscious commitments to the conscious surface and then provide an accountability structure to realize their goals.

Exercise:

Who can you talk and partner with, to elevate your life more intentionally?

#137: "You read a book from beginning to end. You run a business the opposite way. You start with the end, and then you do everything you must to reach it."

– Harold S. Geneen, American businessman

I know a few people who actually read the last chapter of a book to determine if they wish to read the book from the beginning.

Few of us ever want to be told a joke's punch line first, to be told how a sporting event turns out, or to know how a popular movie ends. We like to see how things evolve.

Achieving professional or personal goals is different. We like to ensure a happy, successful ending, and therefore this quote suggests that we begin with the end in mind.

Exercise:

What are your personal and professional goals? Take at least two to three minutes to actually write them down.

Take another two to three minutes to write out steps and milestones along the way that will help you reach them.

Consider doing this exercise with family members, colleagues, or a coach.

#138: "Entrepreneurship is the last refuge of the trouble making individual."

– Natalie Clifford Barney, American writer

There has been a considerable movement in the business world for a good number of years toward entrepreneurship and free agency.

Individuals who take this path have often found that traditional schools and the corporate world were not such a good fit for their authentic desires for professional self-expression. Sometimes these people felt like outcasts, misfits, or even became trouble-makers.

Exercise:

To what degree do you feel aligned with, and fit with, your current vocation?

Even if you choose to stay with this path, how might you venture into a part-time entrepreneurial venture, to find some refuge?

#139: "When you are tough on yourself, life is going to be infinitely easier on you."

– Zig Ziglar, American motivational speaker

In my earlier career as a teacher, a common and often discussed concept was the "bell-shaped curve." This ranked students against one another along a continuum of excellence, where only a select few would obtain the highest ranking. The majority of students ranked in the middle.

In this quote, Zig Ziglar suggests that we as individuals can set our own scale, where our measure of excellence is against ourselves. When we do so, our level of achievement often exceeds what those around us might establish as acceptable or even superior.

Exercise:

Where in your personal and professional life are you coasting, or taking it too easy, because you often still come out toward the front end of the curve?

Select at least one area where you will establish a "boot camp" of intensity and toughness to fully realize your potential.

#140: "Goodwill is the one and only asset that competition cannot undersell or destroy."

– Marshall Field, American entrepreneur

In many ways, I embrace new business strategies and tactics. I have a website that is optimized and updated often. I blog, write, tweet, link, and so on.

Yet in other ways, I'm a bit of an old-fashioned guy. I meet most of my clients in person. I still network face-to-face. I'm a relationship guy.

It often takes considerable time to build trust, goodwill, and loyalty. The value of such goodwill and loyalty has been measured through such sources as Fred Reichheld's book, *The Loyalty Effect* – indicating its value in the billions.

Exercise:

How are your current personal and business practices building the asset of goodwill?

What new and additional ideas will you implement to capture and expand this important asset in the future?

#141: "The employer generally gets the employees he deserves."

– Walter Gilbey, British politician and entrepreneur

A common coaching session I have with individuals in career transition involves the attraction and retention of talent. Once people get beyond specific technical abilities, skill-sets, and experience, we find ourselves shifting from objective decision-making to an emotional decision-making process.

"Will this person have the potential to contribute great value to the organization?" the interviewer thinks.

"Will I be happy, challenged, and rewarded fairly?" the candidate thinks.

The bottom line with both of these forms of thinking is that we are attracted to the future possibility of choosing each other.

Exercise:

If you are an employer, build a company that creates a better future for each employee, and you will get an even better company.

If you are a potential employee, show organizations the future they will get by choosing you to join them.

#142: "You can employ men and hire hands to work for you, but you must win their hearts to have them work with you."

– William J. H. Boetcker, American minister and public speaker

Are you an *employee* or a *team member* where you work?

Do you have a *boss* or a *team leader* that co-ordinates your efforts?

Do you have a vested interest in the work, beyond a paycheck?

Do your days fly by or drag on?

Over the past few years, much has been written and reported about Zappos and how they capture the hearts of both customers and associates. Tony Hsieh (the CEO of Zappos) wrote a book, *Delivering Happiness*, that tells the story of how they do it.

Exercise:

Check out this one-minute video to get a glimpse of what I mean:

www.deliveringhappiness.com/about-us

How can you capture employees' hearts and help them be a part of something bigger?

#143: "To business that we love we rise bedtime, and go to't with delight."

– William Shakespeare, English playwright

What are the qualities and the characteristics of people who love their work and take delight in it? Is it possible to intentionally design work in such a way as to foster greater employee engagement, satisfaction, and productivity?

According to Daniel Pink, in his book, *Drive* (published in 2009), three things are necessary:

Autonomy, which Pink describes as the ability to direct the course of your own life and the work that you perform.

Self-challenge and mastery, or the over-arching desire to improve yourself and get better at what you enjoy.

Purpose, the reason behind your role, beyond personal gain – yes, making a difference through your efforts.

Exercise:

How can you pursue greater autonomy, mastery, and purpose in your work ... and influence your organization to foster these qualities for everyone?

#144: "You have to have your heart in the business and the business in your heart."

– Thomas J. Watson, American businessman

Over 20 years ago, I was faced with a professional fork in the road that eventually, through taking the road less traveled, has had me pursue coaching as my career and professional purpose.

Up until then, I had what many would consider a successful 12-year career in sales, marketing, and advertising with a well-known pharmaceutical company.

Unfortunately, I was unhappy and unfulfilled toward the end. My heart just wasn't in it, and I went into most days with dread and indifference.

Other than marrying my wife, Wendy, and raising two great kids, the pursuit of my passion for coaching is one of the best decisions I've made.

Exercise:

To what degree is your career/business in your heart? What changes can you make to find greater heart in your business?

#145: "No one ever won a chess game by betting on each move. Sometimes you have to move backward to get a step forward."

– Amar Gopal Bose, Indian American entrepreneur and engineer

Recently, my wife and I purchased an iPad and downloaded a puzzle game that we found difficult and frustrating at first. Our attempts to process through the mazes were often thwarted as we attempted to move forward. As we realized that this strategy was not working, we began to explore alternative approaches to achieve our objectives.

Sometimes moving sideways – and often moving backward – are the only strategies that prove successful in the end.

Exercise:

In what ways are your life, career, and relationships like a game of chess, where each move is only a small piece of the puzzle? Where could you move sideways, or even backward, to eventually make forward progress?

#146: "I don't measure a man's success by how high he climbs but how high he bounces when he hits bottom."

– George S. Patton, American general

My dad loves golf. He loves to play it and he loves to watch it. Recently, while watching a tournament together, I noticed the commentator describing the characteristics of a golfer. In talking about him, they used the term "bounce-back factor." This term refers to the ability to achieve a birdie or eagle after a bogey or double-bogey on the previous hole.

Rarely in golf or life do we experience bogey-free rounds or successes without setbacks. Our ability to experience these events and bounce back with resilience and resolve, as Patton suggests, is a measure of success.

Exercise:

How often and how long do you stay down when faced with life's setbacks? What strategies can you employ to bounce back even higher and faster in the future?

#147: "Do not look where you fell, but where you slipped."

– African proverb

Where we fall and where we slip are often not the same place. Slipping always occurs before the fall – and therefore happens at a place where there may be something we can do to potentially prevent the fall.

Consider the following:

- You sense through a body gesture or the tone of someone's voice that an important conversation is headed to an icy patch.

- You step onto the bathroom scale, or your last physical provides you feedback that your health is headed in an undesirable direction.

Exercise:

What clues is your world sending you daily that indicate a fall may be coming? How can you learn to avoid the slippery patches in the first place?

#148: "Great men are rarely isolated mountain-peaks; they are the summits of ranges."

– Thomas W. Higginson, American minister and abolitionist

In July 2012, we vacationed in New Hampshire. We found it to be one of the most beautiful places in New England. During our visit, we experienced the thrill of taking the famous cog railroad up to the summit of Mount Washington, the highest peak in the North-East United States.

Among breathtaking views, we could also view Mount Adams, Mount Jefferson, and many others – all part of the White Mountain range.

Exercise:

Who are some of the great men and women in your life? How have you been part of their greatness?

How have they supported you in being your best? What future great peaks could you pursue together?

#149: "Don't worry that children never listen to you; worry that they are always watching you."

– Robert Fulghum, American author

We have all heard the phrase, "Actions speak louder than words." My wife Wendy and I have been very fortunate to raise two wonderful children who are now on their own as young adults. Although we no longer see them as often as we did when they lived at home, when we do get to visit together, we are pleased to see the effects of many of the lessons we tried to impart throughout the years.

Even though we were not always sure that the messages were getting through, we are delighted to see them living consistently with many of the behaviors we demonstrated through our daily actions.

Exercise:

What do your children and the people in your life observe in your daily actions? How pleased would you be to see them behaving in the same manner?

What adjustments can you make to your actions to have the impact you wish to have?

#150: "When a man is wrapped up in himself, he makes a pretty small package."

– John Ruskin, English artist and art critic

We all know people who are self-centered, egotistical, narcissistic, and arrogant. Most people have at least a trace of these attributes. When we come across people like this, our typical reaction is to withdraw and to avoid them. When people exhibit these behaviors, their worlds become small packages.

When we become far more interested in the lives of others – including family, friends, and colleagues – our world expands exponentially.

Exercise:

How many people would attend your funeral, or attend a party that would celebrate your life?

If the people in your life were to write a eulogy for you, what would you like it to say?

#151: "No person was ever honored for what he received. Honor has been the reward for what he gave."

– Calvin Coolidge, 30th American President

Who are the most honorable people you know and admire? Take a moment and look at the people in your life that you respect and value.

Look at famous people, past and present, great leaders, and humanitarians – you know, the "Who's Who" of mankind. Notice what contributions they made to others, to their communities, and to the world.

Exercise:

How will you use your day to give and contribute more?

Don't be surprised if you happen to receive wonderful things in return.

#152: "Tell me and I'll forget; show me and I may remember; involve me and I'll understand."

– Chinese Proverb

Since my first career as a middle school science teacher in Philadelphia, I have always been fascinated by the process of learning. Back then, the old-school didactic method of teaching did not truly help children to grow in understanding, or to consistently retain information.

As a coach, I engage clients in a multitude of learning experiences, where practical. "On the court" involvement over a six month time frame is critical to long-term understanding.

Exercise:

What professional and personal lessons do you most wish to learn that will make the biggest difference in your life?

How can you build greater involvement and real-world experience into the lessons, to support your desire for greater understanding and long term achievement?

#153: "Though face and form alter with the years, I hold fast to the pearl of the mind."

– Han-shan, Chinese poet

As a society, we put a high priority on what Han-shan calls "face and form". A few months ago, I had the opportunity to see a "Where are they now?" segment on a talk show, where the guests were former highly attractive movie and TV stars.

What I noticed were considerable examples of plastic surgery, and heroic attempts to retain the "face and form" of their youth.

Fortunately, the interviewer focused the conversations around their personal growth and development, as well as their community efforts that went beyond the physical. In these discussions, it was clear that their minds were still beautiful pearls shimmering in the world beyond the surface.

Exercise:

How can you continue to hold fast and further develop your inner self and mind, and see the inevitable process of aging as simply adding a few wisdom lines here and there?

#154: "Yesterday is history, tomorrow is a mystery, and today – today is a gift. That's why we call it the present."

– Babatunde Olatunji, Nigerian drummer and social activist

I'm not big on standing in long lines, even if it is to get a great bargain – and most of my readers know that a great gift for me is a remarkable book, to learn something new, or to have a unique experience.

Fun reflections on the past, and inspiring thoughts about the future, are natural for most of us. However, this quote suggests that we work on being fully present to the "now" that occurs every day.

Exercise:

Purchase a notebook or journal and name it your "Now notebook". Each evening, capture how you lived each day by being fully present to the people, events, and opportunities that occur.

Before going to sleep, spend a moment being grateful that you get to open another wonderful present tomorrow.

#155: "In about the same degree as you are helpful you will be happy."

– Karl Reiland (*attrib.*)

Have you ever noticed that the people who have the most things are often not very happy? Many times, they are downright miserable and no amount of "more" seems to fill their emptiness.

The givers and helpers of the world seem to have a greater sense of contentment and satisfaction with life, even if they come from modest means.

It appears that a life focused on others versus on oneself provides for greater fulfillment.

Exercise:

Experiment by having a "helping day" today where you go out of your way to be extra helpful to friends, family, and colleagues.

Put your random acts of kindness on overdrive and notice the reaction that others have – and just as importantly, notice the many smiles that find their way onto your face.

#156: "Far away there in the sunshine are my highest aspirations. I may not reach them, but I can look up and see their beauty, believe in them and try to follow where they lead."

– Louisa May Alcott, American author

There's an often-quoted goals study from Yale University in 1953 indicating that the 3% of graduates who had clearly-written goals achieved far more than the 97% that didn't. This study has been shown to be fictitious.

There is, however, a study from the Dominican University that shows the following:

1. Those people who wrote their goals down accomplished significantly more than those that did not have written goals.

2. Goal achievement was more likely when accountability was supported by a friend, mentor, or coach.

3. People who also made a public commitment to others achieved more.

Exercise:

Write down your highest aspirations.

Make a public commitment to these goals, and ask someone committed to your success to hold you accountable. You can even call me at 248-740-3231 or email me at barry@dempcoaching.com to tell me about them.

#157: "Keep knocking and the joy inside will eventually open a window and look out to see who's there. These promptings will lead you in certain directions – they're the voices of your heart guiding you in the direction of your destiny. Have the courage to stand in the mystery of your life, and you'll be advancing nicely along your path."

– Rumi, Persian poet

In the summer of 2012, my daughter Rachel began her fifth year working for the Southwestern Company. My understanding is that she and approximately 3,000 college students and young adults participate in this unique profession that few have ever experienced. Their role is to sell educational books "door-to-door" over a 12-week interval. These extraordinary young people work six days each week, often for 14 hours per day.

Talk about knocking and prompting! My wife and I are often dumbfounded at the tenacity it must take to do such a job, literally rain or shine. The result for Rachel has been phenomenal growth and development – she's now a confident, charismatic young woman who can relate to almost anyone.

Exercise:

Where do you need to summon greater courage and take greater initiative to knock on life's doors and advance boldly along your path?

#158: "Life is all about choices. How many people are trapped in their everyday habits: part numb, part frightened, part indifferent? To have a better life we must keep choosing how we're living."

– Albert Einstein, German American theoretical physicist

Since you're reading this book, you likely live in a democratic society where you have the freedom to fully choose how you live each day.

As a coach, I often see individuals who are limiting their freedom to choose. Which of these have you been fully intentional about?

- The choice of career or vocation

- The choice to be healthy and fit

- The choice of friends and associates

- The choice of how you spend your free time

- The choice of where you live, and the communities you associate with

- The choice of your thoughts and attitudes each day

Exercise:

Where are you currently trapped and limited by your everyday habits and thinking? What new and intentional choices can you make to achieve a better life?

#159: "Life is short. Do not forget about the most important things in life, living for other people and doing good for them."

– Attribution uncertain

How much time do we really have? If you live to be 80 years old, you have a total of 960 months – that's 4,160 weeks or 29,220 days.

How many days do you have left to love your family, contribute to others, and make a difference in your personal and professional life?

If you happen to be 40, you either have half of your life behind you – or you have half of your life yet to live.

Exercise:

Given the finite nature of our lives, consider developing a bucket list of 100 things you wish to achieve.

The items on this list that do good for others count twice!

#160: "If there is something to gain and nothing to lose by asking, by all means ask."

– W. Clement Stone, American businessman and philanthropist

A favorite quote from my wife is, "If you don't ask, the answer is no." A related famous Wayne Gretzky quote is, "You miss 100% of the shots that you don't take."

What's the worst thing that could happen if the answer you get is no?

What wonderful results would be possible if you hear "yes" more often than you expect?

Exercise:

Where in your personal or professional life have you been reluctant to ask for what you want?

Place a few Post-it® notes in your work and home with the following phrase, based on the famous Nike slogan: *"Just ask."*

#161: "Life is no brief candle for me. It is a sort of splendid torch which I have got hold of for the moment, and I want to make it burn as brightly as possible before handing it on to future generations."

– George Bernard Shaw, Irish playwright

How often do you find yourself leaping out of bed and looking forward to each day?

How much do you love your work? How extraordinary are your personal and professional relationships? How much adventure and excitement have you experienced recently?

Exercise:

What adjustments and enhancements can you make today in order to set an example of a life burning brightly for others?

#162: "Most people live – whether physically, intellectually or morally – in a very restricted circle of their potential being. We all have reservoirs of life to draw upon of which we do not dream."

– William James, American psychologist and philosopher

Most people discover that the reason they come to engage a coach is to live their lives beyond the restricted circle of their current perceived potential.

By discovering the reality of their own limited views of themselves, they can begin to expand this circle to explore and achieve a level of physical, intellectual, and professional accomplishment that has been previously hidden from them.

Exercise:

To begin to discover the reservoirs of your life:

1. Observe the lives of others who you respect and admire for what they have achieved. Follow their lead.

2. Answer the following "fill-in-the-blank" question:

If I was twice as _____, I would be able to achieve _____.

#163: "Remember that failure is an event, not a person."

– Zig Ziglar, American motivational speaker

As a pioneer in the field of personal and professional development, Zig Ziglar saw clearly that experience – and yes, failure – was a critical factor in achieving success. Here, he is making a critical distinction about failure that retains personal dignity and self-worth, instead of allowing people to feel that they themselves are failures.

My experience is that too many people fear the sting of "being a failure" – so they fail to even attempt new challenges, afraid that they will fall short in their efforts.

Exercise:

Use today to take bold and courageous actions toward your most desired goals, knowing that you are successful – no matter what – simply by making the effort.

#164: "We are capable of greater things than we realize."

– Norman Vincent Peale, American minister and author

Sure, we have all heard similar thoughts from our teachers, parents, colleagues, and friends. We even believe them to some extent. The question to consider here is, "How much more are we actually capable of that is beyond our ability to truly believe?"

If thoughts become things, what must we do with our own thoughts, opinions, judgments, mental models, and yes, personal paradigms, to free us from our own limiting beliefs?

Exercise:

As you think about and create plans for the coming months or years ask the following questions of yourself and of those who know you best:

What am I capable of through the use of my mind?

What am I capable of through the development and use of my body?

What new spiritual developmental opportunities will I take?

#165: "The Universe favors the brave. When you resolve to lift your life to its highest level, the strength of your soul will guide you to a magical place with magnificent treasures."

– Robin S. Sharma, author and leadership expert

www.robinsharma.com

Over the years I have read a number of Robin Sharma's books, including *The Monk Who Sold His Ferrari,* from which this quote was taken.

I fully believe that life itself is a miracle and we as humans have the capacity to manifest our own miracles, to guide ourselves and others to magical places with magnificent treasures.

Exercise:

Consider picking up a copy of Robin's books. Two of his early works are *The Monk Who Sold His Ferrari* and *The Saint, The Surfer And The CEO.* A newer one is *The Leader Who Had No Title.*

Subscribe to his blog for future booster-shots of his thinking and perspective at www.robinsharma.com/blog.

#166: "Be more concerned about making others feel good about themselves than you are making them feel good about you."

– Dan Reiland, American pastor and pastors' coach

www.danreiland.com

I know of few more profound truths than this, to support both personal and professional success.

Focus on others, show genuine interest, truly listen, and let them express themselves freely. Look for the value in their ideas and stop interrupting them to share your next brilliant thought. When you do these things, magic happens.

It's amazing that when people feel good about themselves in your presence, they feel a greater affinity for you as a source of this feeling.

Exercise:

If you email me, barry@dempcoaching.com, with the subject "*Communication Toolbox*", I will send you a free copy of six simple and powerful techniques to take your personal and professional relationships to the next level.

#167: "I have yet to find the man, however exalted his station, who did not do better work and put forth greater effort under a spirit of approval than under a spirit of criticism."

– Charles M. Schwab, American businessman

Carrots or sticks? Encouragement or criticism? It's a choice we make daily at work and at home.

How do you feel when you are acknowledged and encouraged in your efforts? How do you feel when others judge, criticize, and demean your efforts?

It seems that a fundamental human trait is to be right and to make others wrong. Just look at our political parties to see what can occur.

Exercise:

Put on a pair of imaginary "approval glasses", and look at the people around you, and the world, to find out what is good and right.

Share this empowering perspective with others, and help them find their own "approval glasses" to wear.

#168: "If you chase two rabbits, both will escape."

– Anonymous

These days, there seems to be a high value placed on one's ability to multitask to enhance productivity.

The evidence regarding these productivity gains is controversial at best, with many examples of serious downsides – just look at texting while driving a car.

There's no question that focusing on one high-priority task at a time pays huge dividends. There's considerable evidence that most productive people do just that, then move on to the next high-priority task, thus giving the appearance of multitasking.

Exercise:

Use your calendar to break up your day into highly-focused priority items, and take them on one at a time.

If another rabbit comes into your sight, make sure you choose only one to chase. After all, one is far better than none.

#169: "A successful man is one who can lay a firm foundation with the bricks others have thrown at him."

– David Brinkley, American newscaster

People of extraordinary achievement often experience more adversity and judgment than others. The sheer fact that they stand out in the world means that people notice – and often take a shot or two to lower them down a peg.

Somehow, these extraordinary people use these judgments and criticisms to further strengthen their resolve to achieve even more.

Exercise:

How can you use the proverbial bricks thrown at you in your professional and personal life to strengthen your foundation for greater achievement?

Consider your ability to encourage and affirm others as a way to create an even more powerful foundational support for their success.

#170: "It is only possible to live happily ever after on a day-to-day basis."

– Margaret Bonanno, American writer

www.margaretwanderbonanno.com

We are all familiar with the saying, "All great journeys begin with the first step."

Far too many people wish their days, weeks, and even years away by looking into the future for when they expect to be happy – you know, when all the stars align. Unfortunately, for most people, life doesn't seem to work out this way.

Instead, Margaret Bonanno is suggesting we take one bite of life's smorgasbord at a time to experience the bountiful feast that life can be.

Exercise:

What does "Living happily ever after on a day-to-day basis" look like to you?

Consider discussing your thoughts with members of your family, close friends, and with your colleagues at work.

#171: "Find inner peace and thousands will flock to your side."

– Serafim of Sarov, Russian monk

For over 30 years, my professional life has included some form of sales or business development component. The volume of books, tapes, videos, CDs, and DVDs on the subject is enormous – and yet this simple statement may save us all considerable time if we make its message paramount to our efforts.

My interpretation of this idea is that people are attracted to something or someone when they realize that others had a highly favorable experience, or benefit.

Perhaps you remember the scene from the movie *When Harry Met Sally* when the woman across from Meg Ryan and Tom Hanks said, "I'll have what she's having!"

Exercise:

What have you achieved or realized in your life that attracts others to you?

What is it that others have achieved and realized that attracts you to them?

#172: "Cherish your visions and your dreams as they are the children of your soul; the blueprint of your ultimate achievements."

– Napoleon Hill, American self-help author

As a parent, I believe one of our most important jobs is to help develop the capacities of our children to dream and envision a bright and wonderful future.

It is exciting to imagine that we are all born with an inner blueprint that, through our capacity to dream, gets revealed and clarified along life's journey.

This quote is encouraging all of us to exercise the muscles of our soul and fully realize our capacity to grow, in order to express our fully authentic self.

Exercise:

How can you revisit your exuberant and authentic inner child and recapture (or more fully discover) the blueprint of your soul?

Google "vision quest" and consider some of the various means to explore this idea further.

#173: "Persistence prevails when all else fails."

– Unknown

I believe that most people create their own luck, through the work they do day in and day out. This quote suggests that persistence is a key for us to guarantee greater success and achievement.

Unfortunately, persistence almost always looks like work, and the light at the end of the tunnel often appears faint.

Exercise:

A question to ponder is, "Why would we intentionally choose to persist and stay the course?"

Ask yourself, "In what areas of my life does my **'why'** make me cry, or bring me close to tears?" You can bet that you have discovered a domain of your life where both persistence and the resulting rewards of your commitments will be realized.

#174: "The race is not always to the swift ... but to those who keep running."

– Unknown

Over the years, I have known a number of friends, colleagues, and clients who took on the challenge of running a marathon. The most inspiring was a friend named Jerry, who was in his late 40s and about 50lbs. overweight.

Each week of his extensive training program, he would email his friends and colleagues about his efforts and progress. He even gave us his cell phone number to call him during the race, to provide support and encouragement.

The result – Jerry finished the race. (The time? Well, let's say that it was way over six hours.)

Another wonderful result for Jerry is that he now sees he can take on other life challenges, because he keeps putting one foot in front of the other.

Exercise:

What proverbial life races are you planning to run, and where will you need a little "Jerry" inside you in order to finish?

#175: "The foundation stones for a balanced success are honesty, character, integrity, faith, love, and loyalty."

– Zig Ziglar, American motivational speaker

Have you ever tried to cross a small stream on rocks that were sticking out of the water? In my youth, we had this opportunity at summer camp and in the Boy Scouts. We found some of the stones already in place – and in both cases, we needed to place other stones of the appropriate size and shape at the right distance to ensure our successful journey to the other side.

I like Zig Ziglar's choice of foundation stones to stand upon: they are big, solid, and stable.

Exercise:

What additional foundation stones would you add to this list, which will provide you with the additional footholds you need to help you on your journey?

#176: "The older I get the less I listen to what people say and the more I look at what they do."

– Andrew Carnegie, Scottish-American industrialist

Carnegie is famous for wealth creation in the steel industry in the late 1800s, for his extraordinary philanthropic pursuits, and for his interest in education. He was obviously a believer in the fact that talk is cheap and that actions speak louder than words.

One of the statements that I ask my clients to explore prior to beginning a coaching relationship is, "I am known for my courage, integrity, loyalty, and work ethic." This helps us consider the evidence these individuals have for being people of action and not simply of words. Since coaching is all about breaking patterns and taking new and different actions, this quality is critical to success.

Exercise:

On a scale of 1–10 (where 1 = low, 10 = high), how would you rate yourself as a person who truly "walks the talk"?

What will it take to increase your score at least two points – even if this gives you a 12?

#177: "Someday is not a day of the week."

– Unknown

Someone once said that hard work pays off in the future, but procrastination pays off now. This is a funny thought – and it may even be true on a limited basis. However, people who procrastinate and put things off for someday in the future often look back on their lives with regret.

When people are asked about their regrets in their lives, they rarely regret the things they did and often regret the things that they did not do.

Exercise:

Rather than dreaming about the things you will do in the future, consider:

- Traveling to wonderful places
- Starting a business or changing your career
- Learning a new language
- Getting more healthy and fit
- Saving for retirement now
- Engaging in a new hobby

Start – or revisit – your bucket list, developed from the exercise in Quote #159, and place an actual date next to each item on the list.

Try to check one of those items off this week, if possible.

#178: "Opportunities are like sunrises. If you wait too long, you miss them."

– William Arthur Ward, inspirational author

As part of my personal excellence workshop, I often ask my clients, "What inspires you?" Quite often, their answers include aspects of nature, such as beautiful sunrises and sunsets.

How often do you wake before the sun rises, to pursue the opportunities life presents? How often do you sleep in and miss the beauty of the dawn's early light, and the opportunities that go to those early birds?

Some people even go through their days half-asleep, due to their lack of engagement.

Exercise:

How can you live a more inspired and engaged life, and grasp all the beauty and opportunities before you?

Consider doubling the amount of times each day that you say "Yes" and cut the amount of times each day that you say "No" in half.

#179: "Good, better, best. Never let it rest. Until your good is better and your better is best."

– Nursery rhyme quoted by Tim Duncan, American basketball player

Many years ago, I attended a seminar where the leader suggested – very cynically – that the reason most people get up in the morning is because they did not die in their sleep. Wow, what a horrible thought!

This quote from Tim Duncan is why I, and perhaps many engaged, optimistic individuals, get up each morning – to make themselves and their world a bit better, each and every day.

With this sense of purpose, they awake with both the intention and the opportunity to influence their lives for the better.

Exercise:

How can you structure your professional and personal life in order to take what's good and make it better, and take what's already better and make it your best?

#180: "Do your little bit of good wherever you are; it's those little bits of good put together that overwhelm the world."

– Desmond Tutu, South African bishop and opponent of apartheid

www.tutu.org

I have recently finished reading Charles Duhigg's book, *The Power of Habit*. One of the ideas he points out as a way to generate individual and organizational habits that lead to greater success is to focus on "small wins."

Too often we glamorize only the big wins – those Super-Bowl-sized accomplishments that are highlighted in the media – without recognizing all those little steps along the way.

Exercise:

Develop a "little bit of good" journal, scoreboard, or notebook to capture all the ways you can and do make the world a better place.

Create a separate section to capture all the little bits of good others do for you.

Imagine the possibilities of seven billion people doing this exercise!

#181: "People don't buy for logical reasons. They buy for emotional reasons."

– Zig Ziglar, American motivational speaker

I'm not sure if I fully agree with this premise – however, I would support the belief that most buying decisions have a considerable emotional component. Marketers, the media, work associates, and even friends and family are constantly pitching ideas and products. I find that I am most easily sold when both head and heart are involved in the decision – especially when the decisions are big ones.

Consider some of the big decisions that you've made successfully, including such matters as education, location, friendships, environment – and even your life partner. When making decisions such as these, you are unlikely to think, "There is an 83% likelihood we will be married seven years from now." Instead, you pay attention to what your heart says.

Exercise:

How can you listen more closely to the wisdom of your heart, as you consider the decisions you need to make today and in the future?

#182: "The highest reward for a person's toil is not what they get for it, but what they become by it."

– John Ruskin, English artist and art critic

I am a work in progress. How about you? With the wide variety of daily experiences we all have, I believe that we are constantly evolving and becoming a fuller expression of ourselves.

Sure, we all work and toil each day to achieve various forms of compensation that allow us to care for ourselves and others. Ruskin's quote, however, points to the perhaps less recognized and often subtle developments that accompany such experiences.

Exercise:

Explore how your daily efforts further your journey toward more fulfilling relationships, enhance creativity, expand greater self-esteem, support vibrant health, and extend your pursuit of wisdom.

How are you going beyond your basic psychological and physiological needs to pursue your own self-actualization? Consider Googling "Maslow's Hierarchy of Needs" to explore this concept in more depth.

#183: "The most exciting breakthroughs of the 21st century will not occur because of technology, but because of an expanded concept of what it means to be human."

– John Naisbitt, American futurist and author

www.naisbitt.com

In my youth, I found that I often exchanged my time for money. As I get older, I now consider time as a new currency. How I spend my time and who I spend it with has great significance.

I do find that, as a high priority, I spend considerable time exploring and reflecting on life itself, hoping to maximize my potential and to contribute things of significance to those around me.

Exercise:

How can you further develop and expand your concept of what it means to be you?

With this expanded concept in mind, how will you spend your time and who will you spend it with in the future?

#184: "Hard work without talent is a shame, but talent without hard work is a tragedy."

– Robert Half, American businessman

www.roberthalf.com

As a business and personal coach for over 20 years, I have worked with over 1,000 individuals in a wide variety of professions. It is a shame when I see people working 60 hours or more each week in jobs that don't play to their strengths and talents. Many of these people experience high levels of stress, which can sometimes lead to burnout and illness.

As a coach, I help people discover and develop their strengths and unique abilities and apply them in their work. Sometimes, these people have fallen short of their fullest potentials simply because they haven't put in the time and effort to make the most of their abilities.

Exercise:

How can you further discover and develop your talents and put in the work – which hopefully will feel like play – to avoid the tragedy of not realizing your fullest potential?

#185: "Reading one book is like eating one potato chip."

– Diane Duane, American science fiction and fantasy author

www.dianeduane.com

How many of you remember the old Lays potato chip commercial from the 70s and 80s – you know, the one that says you can't eat just one? For some reason, those crispy salty treats caused many of us to find ourselves licking our fingers, having reached the bottom of the bag.

For me, books are a great metaphor for the satisfaction of gaining greater knowledge, entertaining ourselves, and expanding our worlds. They won't even put those extra pounds on you.

Exercise:

Develop a list of books that you intend to read in the coming months. Consider asking your friends, families, and colleagues for their recommendations.

Buy at least one of those books this week on half.com, eBay, or Amazon – and schedule yourself to enjoy those tasty bits of knowledge and pleasure daily.

Please check out my list of book recommendations for more ideas: www.dempcoaching.com/recommended-reading

#186: "The unfed mind devours itself."

– Gore Vidal, American writer

We've all heard the phrase, "You are what you eat." Perhaps this is also the case with our thoughts.

When we feed ourselves positive, affirming ideas and thoughts, our lives expand and become better. When we feed ourselves negative and critical thoughts – which often occur when our minds are not enriched – we tend to regress, becoming smaller and far less fulfilled.

Exercise:

If the phrase, "Thoughts become things", has some truth to it, plan your future cerebral meals carefully to include only the choicest morsels.

Consider purchasing a copy of John Maxwell's *Maxwell Daily Reader* to chew on each day.

Read a passage from the Bible, Torah, Koran, or another inspirational book.

And of course, keep reading this book on a regular basis. You can find more quotes at www.thequotablecoach.com.

#187: "Cease to inquire what the future has in store, and take as a gift whatever the day brings forth."

– Horace, Roman poet

Someone once said that contentment is being satisfied with what you have and who you are. This does not mean that pursing your goals with passion and bettering yourself is a bad idea.

Far too many people spend a considerable amount of time longing for a better future – and often missing life's gifts that happen to be right in front of their noses.

Exercise:

Imagine, as you go through your day, that a wide variety of gifts are being sent to you by some higher power – and even by the people in your personal and professional life.

Make sure that you are wearing your special "gift-seeing glasses" so that you don't miss a single one.

#188: "You'll never really understand a person until you consider things from his point of view ... until you climb inside his skin and walk around in it."

– Harper Lee, American author

One of the pioneers and leaders in the field of personal development, Stephen Covey, passed away in 2012. He was perhaps best known for his classic book, *The 7 Habits of Highly Effective People*. Habit Five states, "Seek to understand and then to be understood."

In our fast-paced world, most of us do an abridged version of this if we do it at all. Lee's quote suggests that we go far deeper and climb under the skin of another to fully understand their perspective and point of view.

Exercise:

When you meet someone you don't know, or even someone you think you know well, try the following three relationship techniques:

1. Ask lots of genuine open-ended questions to show your sincere interest.

2. Take a piece of their answer and use it in your next question, to go deeper and demonstrate that you are truly listening. (This technique is called "layering".)

3. Be silent when they are speaking, so they can fully express their ideas and opinions.

#189: "The universe will fill your cup if you carry a big cup, a little cup, or a thimble."

– Sonia Choquette, American spiritual teacher

www.soniachoquette.com

How full is your life? If it is so full that things are spilling out, perhaps this is because your life vessel is too small, and because some of the wrong things are trying to enter.

This quote points to the importance of the size of our life's vessel, so that it can hold the abundance which the universe can provide. It suggests we have the ability to shift the size from one of limitation to one of greater proportions.

An additional consideration I'd like to suggest is to place a filter over the opening, and let only those people and experiences best suited to your specific life journey enter.

Exercise:

What actions will you take now and in the future both to expand the capacity of your life container and to accept only the highest quality ingredients for a full and happy life?

In other words, go for both: quantity *and* quality.

#190: "Nothing contributes so much to tranquilize the mind as a steady purpose – a point on which the soul may fix its intellectual eye."

– Mary Wollstonecraft Shelley, English novelist

A number of quotes in this book relate to the heart and head regarding decision making. Shelley's quote appears to go even deeper, into the level of soul – our own very being.

I believe she is suggesting that having a steady purpose will provide deeper meaning to our lives and at the same time quiet the loud and often disjointed chatter that frequently occupies our minds.

Exercise:

Block out five minutes each morning when you awake and five minutes each evening before bed to sit in silence with a quiet mind. Focus on or reflect upon your intended purpose for the day.

Take a couple of minutes to capture your thoughts in a purpose log or journal.

Consider discussing these observations or insights with your friends, family, or colleagues over a meal.

#191: "Happiness is a state of consciousness which proceeds from the achievement of one's values."

– Ayn Rand, American political philosopher

The pursuit of happiness is a topic of great interest to most of us. Many people spend considerable time chasing it through the accumulation of material possessions, climbing the corporate ladder, or seeking recognition from others.

Rand may be suggesting that we take off our running shoes and simply look within ourselves for the values that we hold most dear. Once we are clear about these core values, we can then set about our days to live with integrity and passion.

Exercise:

Complete the life vision exercise from Quote #27.

Share this vision, based on your values, with those close to you. Display it at your place of business and in your home as a reminder of your fundamental source of happiness.

#192: "At least three times a day, take a moment and ask yourself what is really important. Have the wisdom and the courage to build your life around your answer."

– Dr. Lee Jampolsky, author of inspirational psychology books

www.drleejampolsky.com

When we want to grow, perhaps the most important quality we can have is full and objective awareness of our current reality, our future vision, and our plans to bridge that gap.

I support Jampolsky's idea of "checking in" morning, noon, and night with what's most important. It's these priorities, when lived with wisdom and courage, which have us live our best life.

Exercise:

Take three 8.5×11 inch pieces of paper and with the largest font possible, write out the phrase, *"What is really important?"*

Place these reminders in those places you are most likely to find yourself in the morning, at noon, and at night.

Feel free to get creative with your smartphone or other digital reminder device, to keep this thought at the forefront of each day.

#193: "It is common sense to take a method and try it. If it fails, admit it frankly and try another. But above all, try something."

– Franklin D. Roosevelt, 32nd American President

In my coaching work with clients, I have a favorite simple technique to help them solve problems. I refer to this as a "pivot point exercise." It involves three simple steps:

1. Identify the current reality of a situation – what's working and not working.

2. Describe your vision for the future that you and others desire.

3. Decide what new and different actions you and others can take that will move you from the current reality toward your committed vision.

Exercise:

Capture this three-step pivot process on a few Post-it® notes and place them strategically in your home and in your place of work.

Add the word "repeat" as the fourth step to build your own self-coaching muscle to move your world forward.

#194: "Courage does not always roar. Sometimes, courage is the quiet voice at the end of the day saying, 'I will try again tomorrow.' "

– Mary Anne Radmacher, American writer and artist

www.maryanneradmacher.net

I love adventure movies – you know, the kind when the hero or heroine summons the courage to overcome seemingly overwhelming odds to reach their goal, get the girl, or achieve some other form of victory.

Radmacher's quote touches home for me in that most of us live much quieter, less adventurous lives, where we summon the courage daily to do our best to contribute and serve others at home and at work.

Exercise:

Consider how often, at the end of your day, you feel the satisfaction of knowing that you did what you could with what you had, where you were.

Capture your thoughts and feelings in a journal or with others.

#195: "Laughter is an instant vacation."

– Milton Berle, American comedian and actor

In his book, *Anatomy of an Illness,* Norman Cousins goes to considerable length to overcome his debilitating condition, with the help of funny movies and other forms of humor, as well as high doses of Vitamin C.

There is considerable evidence that the light-hearted experience of laughter has positive effects on our immune system. It protects our nervous system by reducing stress, and it may actually enhance our life span.

Milton Berle, often referred to as "Mr. Television" or "Uncle Miltie", was born in 1908 and lived to the age of 93; he had a career of bringing mischievous grins and belly laughs to generations.

In our rapidly-moving and often stress-filled lives, we often find ourselves longing for an escape to our favorite vacation spot. Unfortunately, our ability to make these journeys may only occur a few times a year. Let's all take Berle's suggestion, and take far more mini-vacations to brighten our days.

Exercise:

Google Milton Berle and check out some of his video clips on YouTube.

Explore the works of other comedians – such as Lucille Ball, Carol Burnett, Robin Williams, Billy Crystal, and Bob Hope – or check out some funny books and websites and share a few chuckles on a daily basis.

#196: "The only things that stand between a person and what they want in life are the will to try it and the faith to believe it's possible."

– Richard DeVos, American businessman

www.amway.com

Many years ago, I read a book by Wayne Dyer, *Manifest Your Destiny*. In it, Dyer suggests that each person represents a miracle manifested by God – and that since we were created by God, we too have the capacity to create and intentionally manifest our lives.

DeVos is recommending that we exercise our faith muscle and believe that greater things in our lives are possible, and that we can all mobilize our will to take the necessary action to realize these possibilities.

Exercise:

Consider picking up a copy of *Manifest Your Destiny*. I also enjoyed Dyer's book *The Power of Intention*, which you may wish to read as well.

Copy this quote and place it in a prominent place in your world as a reminder (a) to believe that great things are possible and (b) to take the courageous action toward these possibilities each day.

#197: "Enjoy the little things, for one day, you may look back and realize they were the big things."

– Robert Brault, American writer

www.robertbrault.com

The human mind is an amazing thing. It provides us with a phenomenal capacity to learn, to create, to solve problems, and to remember.

There was recently a TV crime show where the detective had a photographic memory – she could remember every single detail. For most of us, this is impossible and in many cases, undesirable. We need to restrict what enters our mind to simply get through our days with a degree of balance and sanity.

Of course we want to remember and cherish those big events, such as graduations, weddings, new jobs, and the births of our children. But, what about those little things – those simple pleasures of each day that add to the richness of life?

Exercise:

Develop a "little things" journal to capture the small and highly important life events that happen each day.

Block out 30 minutes to start your list with at least 100 of these little things, which may actually be the big things that make life so meaningful.

#198: "It's choice – not chance – that determines your destiny."

– Jean Nidetch, American co-founder of Weight Watchers

www.weightwatchers.com

It is surprising to learn the percentage of people who have clearly defined written goals for both their personal and professional life. Estimates are definitely in the single digits – with most hovering around three percent.

So many people have a "take it as it comes" attitude to life, and they may even believe that their destiny is already predetermined. Consider that free will and our capacity to choose how we spend our days are simply fundamental to being human.

Exercise:

Take five minutes this morning to choose how you will spend your day. Select only those activities and people who fit best with your vision and values.

Take five minutes at the end of your day to reflect on what you learned, achieved and experienced.

Consider doing this exercise every day, or at least every week, if you like what you discovered.

Feel free to email me at barry@dempcoaching.com to let me know if something wonderful happens.

#199: "The ability to perceive or think differently is more important than the knowledge gained."

– David Bohm, American theoretical physicist

On/off, right/wrong, black/white are examples of polar opposites or, some might say, the duality of a situation. Knowledge, although highly prized and valuable in our world, often points us in the direction of the "right answer" and can lead us to a somewhat limited view on a particular subject.

Bohm suggests that being open to various perspectives and having the ability to think differently is more important than knowledge in our world today.

Exercise:

Where in your personal and professional life are you limited by knowledge gained and your need to be right? How can you exercise your "try it on" muscle to explore opportunities and possibilities beyond your knowledge of things?

#200: "If we only listened with the same passion that we feel about being heard."

– Harriet Lerner, Ph.D, author of the New York Times bestseller, *The Dance of Anger*

www.amazon.com/The-Dance-Anger-Changing-Relationships/dp/006074104X

My experience in the business of coaching and in a marriage of 34 years has demonstrated to me this key to success. In this quote, Lerner is referring to being "others-focused" versus "self-focused".

Being sincerely interested in others and generously listening so that they can fully express themselves are fundamental to building quality relationships and to leading a successful life.

Exercise:

When you are listening to others with great passion and focus, imagine that money is coming right out of their mouths, and that your job is to capture the full value of what they have to say and contribute.

#201: "The best things in life aren't things."

– Art Buchwald, American humorist

My father used to refer to himself as "one of the richest men around." He had a life filled with the richness of relationships, experiences, community, spirit, faith, purpose and meaningful work.

Many people today feel that they never have enough, and they're always in pursuit of more. But "more" often doesn't make people happier, in spite of what society tells us.

Things cost time. We spend hours not only working to pay for our possessions, but also working to pay to insure, protect, maintain and clean them. We can make the choice to unclutter our lives, hold on to fewer "things", and travel more lightly and simply.

Exercise:

What people and experiences in your life bring you the greatest joy and happiness? To have more of these best things in life, consider scheduling more time with these people, and engage in these activities more often.

#202: "Do not follow where the path may lead; go instead where there is no path and leave a trail."

– Ralph Waldo Emerson, American essayist

We're wired to doing what other people expect of us. We learn (from parents, teachers, and other authority figures) that we should try to fit in and not stand out.

Yet many of us regret that we did not follow our own muse, passions, and visions. Ask yourself:

- What inspires me?
- What am I passionate about?
- Where do I lose all my sense of time?
- Where and when am I the happiest?
- What are my unique abilities and talents?

Exercise:

How will you find the courage to chart your own life journey? Where will you go and what will you do?

Three books that may help you are:

- *Your Best Year Yet*, by Jinny Ditzler
- *Now What? 90 Days to a New Life Direction*, by Laura Berman Fortgang
- *Perfectly Yourself: 9 Lessons for Enduring Happiness*, by Matthew Kelly

#203: "Perpetual optimism is a force multiplier."

– General Colin Powell, American statesman and retired general

Would you describe yourself as an optimist? Optimistic people:

- See the possibilities in things

- Have a "can do" attitude

- See lemonade whenever they see lemons

- Drink from the half-full glass

- Look for the good in everyone

- Find the pony in the room full of dung

- Attract other people and opportunities

Optimism helps us to adjust quickly to adversity: after setbacks, we can get back up faster. By making optimism a habit, you can find something positive in most situations.

Exercise:

Who are the most optimistic people in your world? How can you spend more time with them and be more like them?

Who are the most pessimistic people in your world? How can you reduce their impact, or even remove them from your life?

#204: "The greater danger for most of us lies not in setting our aim too high and falling short, but in setting our aim too low and achieving our mark."

– Michelangelo, Italian artist

I guess spending five years painting the ceiling of the Sistine Chapel is an example of reaching consistently for new heights. In fact, most of Michelangelo's works are examples of extraordinary achievements.

- What have been your proudest moments in life?
- Where have you dared to achieve greatness, or a higher purpose?
- How did stretching or reaching for these seemingly out of reach goals help you grow?

Exercise:

Where in your professional or personal life are you playing too small and too safe?

What goals in your life are worth greater risk, even the risk of failure?

#205: "Time is the coin of your life. It is the only coin you have, and only you can determine how it will be spent."

– Carl Sandburg, American poet and author

When we are young, we believe that we have an unlimited amount of time. Who cares if we waste a day, a week, a month, or even a year? We trade our time for money, and as we pine for more and more things, we often get caught up in a vicious cycle. It starts to feel as if time is running out.

If you're lucky enough to live for 82 years, how many hours will that be? How many days? How many weeks? How many months? When you do the math, you can work out what an hour, day, week, month, or year is truly worth to you.

82 years works out to around 30,000 days. That's 4,200 weeks, and less than 1,000 months. If you're 40 years old, you have around 500 months left.

Exercise:

Imagine a big jar with 4,200 quarters. Each week, you take one quarter out. That's your life being used up. What changes will you make today to spend your time more wisely?

#206: "I long to accomplish a great and noble task but it is my chief duty to accomplish humble tasks as if they were great and noble."

– Helen Keller, deaf-blind American author and activist

People know me as a bit of a junkie for anything to do with personal growth and development. I encourage my clients to reach for the highest heights, realize their visions, and turn their dreams into reality.

And yet life doesn't always look this way. We all have chores to do, meals to prepare, beds to make, and even, for me, cat litter to clean up.

This quote helped me not to struggle with the seemingly small and menial tasks of life. At the end of each day, when I shift from being a business leader and coach that top people come to, I clean the kitty litter, change the water, and make sure the cats' world is OK.

I could pay someone else to do that for me – but I find some nobility, honor, and humanity in serving these little creatures.

Exercise:

Where can you shift your perspective and find nobility and greatness in your small, daily tasks, as well as in the grander moments of your life?

#207: "We build too many walls and not enough bridges."

– Sir Isaac Newton, English physicist and mathematician

Walls separate and protect; bridges join and connect. What walls have you built around yourself, your family, or your organization to seemingly protect yourself? You may have found that they actually separate you from others, to the point of disconnection, loneliness, and seclusion.

We live best in community, and bridges help us come together to create more than we can manage alone.

Exercise:

What are the bridges you need to build or repair?

What are the walls in your life that need to be lowered or torn down?

#208: "A man only learns in two ways, one by reading, and the other by association with smarter people."

– Will Rogers, American actor

I love to learn: it is one of my signature strengths. I take a great interest in the world of blogging and books, because they constantly feed this passion.

A book, for me, can be a source of crystallized wisdom from someone I may have never met, who took the time to share their knowledge, insight, and perspective of perhaps many years.

Exercise:

Who are the people in your world (that may not necessarily be smarter than you) who have much to contribute? How committed are you to having open ears and an open mind?

#209: "We are what we repeatedly do. Excellence, then, is a habit."

– Socrates, classical Greek philosopher

Over 95% of New Years' resolutions never come to pass. There seems to be too much life inertia that keeps things much the same. When change does come, it's often from outside us ... and it's often unwelcome.

Exercise:

Here's a simple three step process to bring the discipline of personal excellence into your life:

1. List two or three things you really, really desire.

2. Identify the vital behaviors that are essential to achieving these things.

3. Engage in these behaviors every day for at least three weeks (more is better). Design as many social and structure supports as you can, in order to help you stay the course.

#210: "A pessimist sees the difficulty in every opportunity, an optimist sees the opportunity in every difficulty."

– Winston Churchill, British Prime Minister

Call it attitude, perspective, a paradigm, or a mental model: how we look at things affects everything. The lenses we wear as we look at life truly color what we see.

I tend to lean heavily in the direction of optimism and possibilities. I seek moments of learning when things do not go the way I desire.

Most people like to be around others with a can-do, find-a-way perspective.

Exercise:

What strategies can you develop to see good things in life as the norm, and the not-so-good things as temporary barriers to overcome?

#211: "A bad habit never goes away by itself: it's always an 'undo-it-yourself' project."

– Pauline Phillips, American advice columnist ("Dear Abby")

Many researchers would say that we are our habits, good or bad. Depending on your age, you have 20, 30, 40, or more years of practice engaging in your bad habits – no wonder they seem so resistant to change.

Exercise:

Begin your "undo-it-yourself" project by replacing a bad habit with a good one, using the following four steps:

Step #1: Select a bad habit you wish to break which is keeping you from a high-priority goal.

Step #2: Identify the new habit you desire by observing individuals who've achieved this goal.

Step #3: List the exact behaviors they consistently engage in and copy their effort as closely as possible for at least three weeks.

Step #4: Enlist additional social and structural support to ensure your success.

#212: "Have patience. All things are difficult before they become easy."

– Saadi, Persian poet

A common characteristic of hard-driving "type A" people is impatience. Often, this quality leads to considerable success. It can, however, also have a dark side.

I'm currently reading Susan Cain's book, *Quiet: The Power of Introverts in a World That Can't Stop Talking*. There's considerable evidence from her research that introverts frequently demonstrate greater patience and often greater mastery of tasks that require patience and persistence.

Exercise:

In what areas of your personal and professional life would greater patience support greater success?

Watch Cain's TED talk, "The Power of Introverts", at:

www.ted.com/talks/susan_cain_the_power_of_introverts.html

Or consider reading the book, if you have the patience.

#213: "Follow effective action with quiet reflection. From the quiet reflection will come even more effective action."

– Peter Drucker, American management consultant and author

One of the most important elements of a coaching relationship is the gift of feedback. Many (if not most) of life's greatest lessons occur following experiential learning, rather than head or book lessons.

Drucker, who is considered by many as one of the great pioneers of modern leadership and management, knew this well over the course of his distinguished career.

Exercise:

Practice the following three-step self-coaching exercise to gain greater insight into your efforts and increase your effectiveness:

Step #1: Ask yourself what is working and not working regarding your current efforts.

Step #2: Reflect on what your desired goal or outcome is beyond the current status.

Step #3: Brainstorm alone or perhaps with a friend or colleague some new or different actions that will likely get you to your goal.

Feel free to repeat this process as often as needed.

#214: "I get a chance to be anyone I want to be."

– Johnnetta McSwain, American author

www.johnnettamcswain.com

As many people know, Oprah has had a phenomenal career of over 25 years, living by the motto, "Live your best life." McSwain's quote points us to the opportunity to be whoever we wish.

One way to explore the possibility of your best future self is to identify people who you respect and begin to practice and express their most admirable skills and qualities.

Exercise:

Develop a list of three to five people in both your professional and personal life, and capture the admirable qualities about each of these individuals. Consider sharing your intentions with each of these people so that they can support your development.

A bonus result will be an improved relationship with these individuals, due to the acknowledgement they will likely experience.

#215: "There is, indeed, something inexpressibly pleasing in the annual renovation of the world, and the new display of the treasure of nature."

– Samuel Johnson, English author, literary critic and lexicographer

We are in late spring in Michigan, and it is sure a sight to see. With some much-needed rain, it appears that all the trees, grasses, and flowers just took a big drink and decided to put on a full show of their beauty.

For me, this vivid display is a huge eye-opener – however, I've realized that it takes a veritable explosion of such beauty to get my attention.

Exercise:

Take at least a full minute each day to fully take in the treasure of nature – no matter how big or small. I hope this small act will provide you with a boost of inspiration and passion that lasts throughout your day.

Consider displaying photographs of nature at work and home and perhaps bring a bit of nature indoors to enjoy.

#216: "When we are no longer able to change a situation, we are challenged to change ourselves."

– Viktor Frankl, Austrian psychiatrist and Holocaust survivor

Very few days pass by without each of us experiencing several upsets. It is very common for our desires to be unfulfilled or our expectations to be thwarted by outside events. One way to navigate these bumps in the road is to look inward at our attitudes, so we can maintain our footing and continue to move ahead.

Exercise:

What are a few upsetting or undesirable situations in your professional or personal life that you are unable to change at this time?

What do you need to do to rise to the challenge of changing yourself, in order to make the best of these difficult circumstances?

#217: "A possibility is a hint from God. One must follow it."

– Søren Kierkegaard, Danish philosopher

How often do you dream or daydream? How often do you ask yourself questions that begin with, "What if...?", "How can I ...?", or simply, "What's possible here?"

Martin Luther King, Jr., had a dream. John F. Kennedy saw a man going to the moon. Orville and Wilbur Wright saw man-made flight become a reality.

Man is a journeyer; our species has a restless urge to go beyond its limits. What about you?

Exercise:

Each morning, ask and answer the question, "What is possible today?"

Take a moment to choose at least one of your answers and follow it.

Feel free to share with me what successes you achieve, by emailing barry@dempcoaching.com.

#218: "If you won't be better tomorrow than you were today, then what do you need tomorrow for?"

– Rabbi Nachman of Breslov, founder of the Breslov Hasidic movement

Most individuals who seek the assistance of a coach have a strong, fundamental desire for growth and development. Being their best, realizing their full potential, and testing their limits are common values these people tend to share. To what degree are you still a work in progress, even if you are many years beyond any formal education?

Exercise:

Explore the list below to assess your progress so far, or your desire to work on these today to have some better tomorrows:

- Parenting
- Health and fitness
- Career advancement
- Faith
- Hobbies
- Music and art
- Friendship
- Leadership
- Emotional intelligence
- Home repair

#219: "You will never stub your toe standing still. The faster you go, the more chance there is of stubbing your toe, but the more chance you have of getting somewhere."

– Charles Kettering, former head of research at General Motors

I've been learning about the differences between introverts and extroverts in relationship to their various routes to achievement. Given the quote above, you would be correct in assuming that extroverts would probably stub their toe more frequently. Introverts tend to be a bit more cerebral and cautious about the steps they take, to apparently avoid some missteps.

Regardless of whether you are an introvert or extrovert, Kettering emphasizes the need to act if we wish to move our lives forward.

Exercise:

Ask friends, family members, and colleagues for feedback regarding your propensity for action. Are you more of a ready-aim-shoot or a ready-shoot-aim person? Hopefully you are not a ready-aim-aim-aim-aim individual!

#220: "It is by spending oneself that one becomes rich."

– Sarah Bernhardt, French actress

About six or seven years ago, I attended a coaching conference where one of the keynote speakers was Lynne Twist. Lynne is a global activist and fundraiser who had the audience enthralled with amazing stories and encounters from her work.

Her book, *The Soul of Money*, offers many revealing insights into our attitude toward money in regard to earning it, spending it, and yes, giving it away as a means of expanding our prosperity.

Exercise:

One of the quotes in this book is, "Time is the coin of your life", by Carl Sandburg. With this in mind, how can you spend yourself and your time each day – and in the process, become richer for it?

Consider picking up a copy of *The Soul of Money* to see what insights it may hold for you.

#221: "An uneasy conscience is a hair in the mouth."

– Mark Twain, American author and humorist

In the earliest days of my coaching career, only a couple of months after I left my job in the pharmaceutical industry, I joined a small consulting firm. Their unofficial motto regarding income generation was, "You eat what you kill" – and unfortunately, I was starving. Of course, if we did "kill" anything, we had an agreement to share a portion of our income with the house.

After about 90 days with absolutely no income, my first client gave me a personal check in my name for $1,000. I kept that check in my wallet for almost a week, unsure if I should share it with the company who – up to that point – compensated me only with a key to the door and permission to use the telephone.

To say I had an uneasy conscience was putting it mildly. I actually made myself ill to the point of vomiting due to my internal conflicts. Living by the quote, "The truth will set you free", I discussed this issue openly with my colleagues – and I was almost instantly healed.

Exercise:

Where in your personal or professional life are you faced with an uneasy conscience, where summoning the courage of your integrity will remove the hair from your mouth?

#222: "The potential that exists within us is limitless and largely untapped ... when you think of limits, you create them."

– Robert J. Kriegel and Louis Patler, American business authors

www.kriegel.com

Recently, I saw the movie *Star Trek: Into Darkness*, directed by J.J. Abrams. As an original fan of the series, I love the idea of boldly going where no man has gone before.

A key characteristic of Captain James T. Kirk is that he constantly challenges his limits, when those around him seem to insist on them. This quality is perhaps why we find his character so appealing. We, too, wish to have more excitement and adventure, to spice things up.

Exercise:

Where are you currently limiting yourself in your thinking and actions? If some of these limits were removed, where could you boldly go today and in the future?

#223: "All meaningful and lasting change starts first in your imagination, then works its way out."

– Albert Einstein, German-American theoretical physicist

One of my favorite quotes is, "When patterns are broken, new worlds will emerge," by Tuli Kupferberg.

Here, Einstein is pointing to our imagination muscle as a means of creating these new worlds. In fact, the definition of imagination is *the faculty or action of forming new ideas, images, or concepts not currently present.*

Exercise:

Select a five-minute break in your day for an "imagination vacation" to tap into your creativity and expand your resourcefulness.

#224: "One's first step in wisdom is to question everything – and one's last is to come to terms with everything."

– Georg Christoph Lichtenberg, German scientist and satirist

When is the last time you spent an hour (or more) with a young child? Parents know all too well the litany of questions that can be generated. These little ones are sponges beginning their wisdom journeys, and can renew our own inspiration to be lifelong learners.

Often our questions far outnumber our answers, and it's not unusual to be upset or even knocked off our games because of this imbalance. Coming to terms with life seems to come with maturity and leads to far greater wisdom – which can help us experience far greater contentment and peace.

Exercise:

What is the right balance of curiosity and acceptance of the world around you that will lead you to the personal wisdom you desire?

#225: "Today is when everything that's going to happen from now on begins."

– Harvey Firestone Jr., American businessman

A considerable number of people who enter into a coaching relationship have a "governor" on their life and career engine that seems to be limiting them from moving forward at the speed they desire.

Their trips down memory lane regarding past accomplishments and setbacks often limit what they're willing to do at this moment in time.

Exercise:

To minimize these journeys into the past, which may limit your forward movement, consider creating a number of Post-it® notes with the following question. Place them throughout your personal and professional environments.

What is the most important thing I can do at this very moment?

Repeat this question often, to do what you can from where you are.

#226: "There ain't no rules around here! We're trying to accomplish something!"

– Thomas Edison, American inventor

How often have you noticed that many projects take quite a bit longer to complete than expected? Sometimes these efforts are thwarted by organizational complexity and misalignment and never see the light of day.

I fully support the use of appropriate systems and procedures when there is alignment among the group. This is often not the case, however, and issues remain unresolved due to the underlying disagreements.

Exercise:

Next time you are part of a committee, task force, or project team that's having difficulty getting something across the goal line, try using the following technique:

Step #1: Ask, "What do you think we should be doing differently, that would work better?"

Step #2: Try on the ideas of others to see if you can align with their suggestions.

Step #3: If for some reason you don't align with their suggestions, make a counter-proposal and start again.

This iterative process will have the group challenge out-dated or dysfunctional rules – and hopefully get it back on the road to greater accomplishment.

#227: "To know the road ahead, ask those coming back."

– Chinese proverb

As a coach, one of the common projects I help people with is starting a new business.

Approximately 80% of business efforts fail in the first five years. Starting a business can be both an exciting and scary time. Thoughts such as, "What if this happens..?", "I don't know how to...", and general fears of the unknown often cause lots of false starts and second-guessing.

The good news is that few new ventures are without examples of people who've "been there and done that."

Exercise:

Do your homework well before you jump into the deep end, and study the efforts and outcomes of others who've gone before you. This way, you can take the good and leave the bad on your journey.

To dramatically improve your odds, I strongly suggest you seek the support of mentors, coaches, and supporters with a track record of success.

#228: "A 'coach' remains something or someone who carries a valued person from where they are to where they want to be."

– Kevin Hall, American business consultant and author

Someone I admire once mentioned to me that when we define something, we limit it, and when we distinguish something, we open up the possibilities of what it can be.

Hall, in this quote, appears to be distinguishing the word "coach" as either a person, an event, or thing that helps you go from where you are to where you want to be. The attribute of "caring for another" is also inherent in his understanding of the word.

Exercise:

Who are the people in your life that act as support structures for you, helping you to get where you want to be?

What are the things in your world that also act as supportive coaches and assist and support your journey?

Make some efforts this week to both acknowledge the coaches and to expand this list beyond its current scope.

#229: "I have one life and one chance to make it count for something ... My faith demands that I do whatever I can, wherever I am, whenever I can, for as long as I can, with whatever I have, to try to make a difference."

– Jimmy Carter, 39th American President

Jimmy Carter sums up a fundamental need (and value) that most people have. His life is a very strong example of fulfilling the need to contribute and to make a difference. Even at the age of 89, he still puts forth his best in support of a variety of causes that have great meaning and purpose.

Exercise:

Where are today's opportunities for you to do whatever you can to make a difference in your world?

Taking into account your health status and your capabilities, what are some of the longer-range goals that you will commit to, so that you can leave a legacy of contribution?

#230: "How far you go in life depends on your being tender with the young, compassionate with the aged, sympathetic with the striving, and tolerant of the weak and strong. Because some day in your life you will have been all of these."

– George Washington Carver, American scientist and inventor

As I write this at my current age of 56, I find myself often reflecting on my life and on those around me. I consider myself fortunate to be aware of myself and my world as I support others through coaching.

In the past few months, I've interacted with babies, seen young teens celebrate their B'nai Mitzvah, celebrated my son's marriage, partnered with many middle-aged individuals in a variety of professional and personal challenges, and partnered with my wonderful wife in supporting my aging father.

Exercise:

What stage of life do you find yourself in, and how can you partner with those around you to appreciate and generously contribute to all the people you meet along the way?

#231: "The heart that gives, gathers."

– Marianne Moore, poet and writer

When I began my coaching career over 20 years ago, the primary method I used to build my business was networking. Of course, this was at the early stages of the internet and social media was about a decade away from seeing its first light.

Networking, when practiced most effectively, emphasizes giving before gathering. In fact, if you try to gather first, it most often backfires. The premise of giving is that it both feels right and often generates a desire from the other person to reciprocate in kind.

Exercise:

1. Focus, in the coming weeks, on generously contributing to members of your networks.

2. Go out of your way to meet new people, who may at some point be valuable additions to yourself and your existing network.

Don't count on it, but don't be surprised when you reap the rewards of reciprocity.

You can get a free copy of my Masterful Networking workbook here:

www.dempcoaching.com/download-your-free-workbooks

The password is **barrydemp** (all lower-case). This also gives you access to my other two workbooks.

If you have difficultly downloading the workbook, please email me at barry@dempcoaching.com with the words "Masterful Networking" in the subject line and I will send you a copy.

#232: "To keep a lamp burning, we have to keep putting oil in it."

– Mother Teresa, Indian Nobel Peace Prize winner

To keep our bodies going, we must put food and water into them. To keep our cars running, we must put fuel into them. To keep our appliances running, we must plug them into an energy source.

Exercise:

Beyond food and water, what is your proverbial oil that keeps you burning? Consider selecting from the list below – and feel free to add your own ideas:

- Quality of relationships

- The pursuit of knowledge and wisdom

- Religious and faith-based practices

- Meaningful goals that inspire your passion and efforts

- Commitment to community and country

- A journey toward personal mastery

- Helping or being of service to others

#233: "One can choose to go back toward safety, or forward toward growth. Growth must be chosen again and again; fear must be overcome again and again."

– Abraham Maslow, American psychologist

What would you do today if you were laid off from your job unexpectedly? Most of us would be jolted from our experience of relative stability into full alert, maybe even panic.

On the other hand, what if each morning, you had a new job or career, where you got to lead and influence your day? What new results and difference could you make? It's up to you to pursue safety or growth, courage or fear. Your choice!

Exercise:

As you go throughout your day, reflect on the following thoughts:

Faced with "X", I usually do "Y". Instead, I'm going to choose "Z" which will support my growth.

#234: "What becomes fragile when we age is not our bodies as much as our egos. The best time to take some daring steps is when we get older."

– Helen Hayes, American actress

Often, I am asked by my clients, "Who are your coaches? Who supports you in living your best life?"

Over the years, I've had a number of key people who have supported me. The best and most enduring has been my 87-year-old father, Marvin. For over 57 years, he has been a steadfast supporter.

In the year following my mom's passing, my father, my wonderful wife Wendy and I engaged in the following:

- A hot air balloon ride
- A safari in the Animal Kingdom at Disney World
- A high-speed adventure on the Test Track ride at Epcot
- A trip to the top of Mount Washington, the highest peak on the Eastern US Coast, on the famous Cog Railroad
- A canoe ride down the Delaware River

Exercise:

Regardless of your age, how can you find a bit more daring and adventure to spice up your life, and engage others you care about in the journey?

#235: "You may have a fresh start at any moment you choose. This thing we call 'failure' is not the falling down, but the staying down."

– Mary Pickford, Canadian-American actress

Whenever I'm asked about the value of coaching, I usually say that people who have a coach almost always achieve more than they would on their own, faster than they would on their own. One key reason for this is that they get up more quickly following the setbacks that often occur when they stretch beyond their comfort zones.

A coach supports the propensity for committed action and will often provide a hand – or even a kick in the butt if necessary! – to help people get up, brush away the dust of apparent failure, capture the lessons learned, and get right back to it.

Exercise:

Select a setback or failure you recently experienced and discuss it with a close friend or colleague. Request their coaching or support to "get right back on the horse" and try again.

Schedule frequent touch-points with this person, so that if you stumble again, you bounce back more quickly and give it another go.

#236: "I have lived a long life and had many troubles, most of which never happened."

– Mark Twain, American author and humorist

Do you know anyone who worries a lot? These individuals are often people who experience considerable fear throughout their lives. Perhaps you are one of them.

Twain points to the fact that many of these fears and worries are unfounded – and yet they limit our enjoyment of life considerably.

Exercise:

When you, or someone you know, is experiencing worry or fear, ask yourself or the other person these questions:

1. What is the likelihood that this thing I'm afraid of will actually happen?

2. What if I am successful?

3. Who can help me resolve this?

4. What one step can I take to improve the situation?

5. What, realistically and objectively, is the worst that could happen?

6. How would I cope with it if it did?

7. What can I do to minimize the danger of ... ?

Lastly, try breathing deeply. This technique has a magical way of lightening the load of worry.

#237: "If you judge a fish by its ability to climb a tree, it will live its whole life believing it's stupid."

– Albert Einstein, theoretical physicist

We often spend too much time focusing on weaknesses at the expense of strengths. Who hasn't, as a child, had a parent review their report card and make strong suggestions to improve the Ds and Cs toward As and Bs?

Unfortunately, this produces a double-whammy for the student. They usually lack the desire to work on these areas, and this parental feedback fosters their belief in their inadequacy and even stupidity regarding the subject.

Instead of working on our weaknesses, we will achieve much more by playing to our strengths and fanning the flames of a fire that's already burning.

Exercise:

If fish gotta swim and birds gotta fly, what areas of natural talent and ability can you develop in yourself to realize your own genius?

#238: "It is better to be prepared for an opportunity and not have one than to have one and not be prepared."

– Whitney Young, Jr., American Civil Rights Leader

When I was young, I was a Boy Scout – a member of that organization that teaches young people to "be prepared." Although I never achieved the rank of Eagle Scout, this motto has remained with me all these years.

People today may tease or ridicule us for being a Boy Scout – for the plans we make, the lists we create, and the forethought we give to projects and areas of importance. For me, being a bit of a Boy Scout has worked out pretty well.

Exercise:

Look at your own efforts to be prepared for those important opportunities you may know about – and perhaps others not currently on your radar.

Determine what additional or modified Boy Scout habits would help you make the most of the opportunities life presents.

#239: "Your network is your net worth."

– Tim Sanders, American business author

www.timsanders.com

In recent years, I've been amazed that a good number of large companies have paid billions of dollars to acquire various social media sites. A critical key to the value of these social media sites are their networks of millions of users and customers.

Someone once told me that if I was to square the number of people in my network, it would be highly correlated to my net worth. That's right: if you have 1,000 people in your network, your net worth would be $1,000,000.

I know this sounds very simplistic; however, I continue to see much value in my own use of tools such as LinkedIn for business networking and ACT! as my Customer Relationship Management software.

Exercise:

Do your own network assessment to see its current valuation. Should you wish to grow it further, consider downloading my free workbook on Masterful Networking:

www.dempcoaching.com/download-your-free-workbooks

The password is **barrydemp** (all lower-case). If you have difficultly downloading the workbook, email me at barry@dempcoaching.com and I will send you a copy.

Also, consider reading some of Tim Sanders' work, including *Love is the Killer App,* and *The Likeability Factor.*

#240: "A single conversation with a wise man is worth a month's study of books."

– Chinese proverb

One definition of wisdom, crowd-sourced by Wikipedia, is *a deep understanding and realization of people, things, events, or situations resulting in the ability to apply perceptions, judgments, and actions in keeping with this understanding.*

Wisdom embraces fundamental human principles, including the capacity to reason, the use of knowledge, and the ability to determine one's path forward. The coaching process often ventures deeply into the realm of wisdom – for both the student and the coach.

Coaching, like the reading of great books (which, as you know, I highly recommend), results in the enhanced creativity, insight, and collaboration that happens when two minds focus together on a single matter.

Exercise:

Create a short list of wise men and women that currently support or could support your personal mastery journey.

Select at least one individual in your world who would benefit from the contribution of your wisdom.

#241: "If you can tell me who your heroes are, I can tell you how you're going to turn out in life."

– Warren Buffett, American businessman and philanthropist

While doing a bit of research on Buffett's interesting upbringing and career, I learned that he was highly influenced by a prominent investor of his time, named Ben Graham.

Ben is noted for creating the concept of intrinsic business value, which represents an alternative way to determine the value of a company. As one of the world's richest men, Buffett obviously was inspired by his hero to follow his teachings.

Exercise:

Who are your heroes? What values, behaviors, and wisdom do they possess that would cause you to model your own life after them?

Consider the idea that you are someone's hero. How will you continue your own growth journey to be the kind of person worth following?

#242: "At the end of each day, you should play back the tapes of your performance. The results should either applaud you or prod you."

– Jim Rohn, American entrepreneur and motivational speaker

www.jimrohn.com

The gift of feedback from others, and the insights gained through self-reflection, are critical to coaching success. Without them, as Rohn notes, we are not sure if we are to celebrate our efforts or double-down to try something new on our next attempt.

Exercise:

Ask yourself the following questions at the end of your day, regarding your efforts in your personal and professional life:

1. What worked well that pleased you, and how can you build on that success tomorrow?

2. What did not work out today as you expected, and what new and different actions can you take tomorrow that would bring you the results you desire?

Consider asking these questions for a week and see if the habit of a daily playback improves your performance.

#243: "Try to be like the turtle – at ease in your own shell."

– Bill Copeland, Australian athlete

Turtles and tortoises are interesting creatures. Below are a few facts:

1. They actually make a sound, even though they do not have vocal chords.

2. Tortoises orbited the moon before astronauts did, in the Soviet space probe Zond 5.

3. They don't have ears – but can perceive low-pitched sounds.

4. They are nearly as old as the dinosaurs, with examples going back over 200 million years.

5. They can see color and have a preference for red, orange, and yellow.

Exercise:

Take a few moments to look within yourself and discover the wonders of you, to be at ease in your own shell.

If this is a bit challenging, consider requesting such feedback from those close to you.

#244: "The great secret of success is to go through life as a man who never gets used up."

– Albert Schweitzer, German / French humanitarian

Albert Schweitzer was born in Germany in 1875. In his life of 90 years, he had many occupations, including philosopher, scholar, doctor, musician, missionary, preacher, theologian, and journalist. His primary life objectives included the brotherhood of nations and helping solve the world's problems.

In 1952, he received the Nobel Peace Prize for his philosophy of "Reverence for Life."

Exercise:

Imagine you have just been honored with your own Nobel Prize for your contribution to your professional and personal worlds. What would you like your success legacy to include?

#245: "It's on the strength of observation and reflection that one finds a way."

– Claude Monet, French impressionist painter

This past summer, I had the opportunity to visit the Museum of Fine Arts in Boston, and saw some of Monet's work. It is said that he rejected traditional approaches to landscape painting and instead of copying old masters, he began learning from nature itself. He particularly took note of variations of color and light caused by daily or seasonal changes.

Exercise:

How can you find your own way to live your life and pursue your goals on your own strength of observation and reflection?

Consider checking out Daniel Pink's book, *A Whole New Mind*, published in 2005, to exercise your right brain in what's still a pretty left-brained world.

#246: "The first to apologize is the bravest. The first to forgive is the strongest. And the first to forget is the happiest."

– Unknown

Recently, I have been working with my friend and personal organizer Lisa, to help remove some clutter from my home. It is amazing the happiness I experience to see my junk drawers open easily and to enter my closet where I have only the clothing that fits me. Donating those items I was not using felt pretty good too.

When I saw this quote, it made me think of the mental and emotional clutter we often carry around with us – and how this area can often benefit from a bit of a makeover.

Exercise:

Consider picking up a copy of *The Happiness Project* by Gretchen Rubin, where she describes her year-long journey using a wide variety of strategies to become happier.

#247: "Genius is no more than childhood recaptured at will."

– Charles Baudelaire, French poet and translator

I just did a Google search for the top ten most influential people of all time. Who do you think was number one on this list? Jesus. Others included Muhammad, Gandhi, Buddha, Confucius, and of course, Einstein.

In her book, *Jesus CEO* (written in 1992), Lauri Beth Jones identifies over 80 key characteristics of how Jesus lived his life. One quality I particularly like was his ability to be playful and share his sense of humor, spontaneity, and joy. His genius helped others lower their defenses and flock to be with him.

Exercise:

I strongly encourage you to pick up a copy of Jones' book and review at least one of Jesus' qualities each day.

Each section will only take about three minutes to read but may take quite a bit longer to reflect and act upon. I assure you, it will be worth it.

#248: "The mind is not a vessel to be filled but a fire to be kindled."

– Plutarch, classical Greek historian

In his book, *Outliers: The Story of Success,* Malcolm Gladwell shares his unique perspective and findings in the areas of what makes people successful. Surprisingly, there appears to be no significant correlation between high intelligence (even genius) and long term success. Once someone reaches an IQ of around 120, having additional IQ points doesn't seem to translate into a measurable real-world advantage.

I'd like to suggest that once the mind is filled sufficiently, it triggers some reaction to mobilize one's heart and spirit to pursue a passionate quest for one's path through life.

Exercise:

Explore your daily activities to see what experiences, people, and yes, knowledge and wisdom, light your fires of life.

Consider making more time for these by stopping what you can in order to make room for them.

#249: "The merit of originality is not novelty; it is sincerity."

– Thomas Carlyle, Scottish philosopher and writer

One of the cornerstones to the value of coaching is the stickiness or sustainability of success that it provides.

An example of stickiness can be found in brand loyalty, to specific products and services that have stood the test of time.

Think about your own loyalty to specific brands, even when faced with the onslaught of novel and often catchy campaigns attempting to lure you away from these sincere and enduring relationships. To borrow a phrase used by one of the most successful brands in the world, we are looking for "the real thing."

Exercise:

Take a few quiet moments to write out your own original vision statement, based on your most sincerely held beliefs and values.

Consider doing this exercise with close friends or family members, to embrace the mutual merits of each person's originality.

For example, *"My Life Vision is a healthy, peaceful, beautiful world of extraordinary relationships, great accomplishments, and integrity; an exciting world of respect, dignity, leadership, courage, and honor, where all people generously and passionately contribute their best to one another."*

#250: "We write to taste life twice: in the moment and in retrospection."

– Anais Nin, American author

One of the habits that both supports and expedites results achieved during a coaching relationship is journaling.

Using some form of log book to capture tools used, lessons learned, and insights revealed is like doing more reps at the gym or taking extra practice sessions in your favorite sport to build greater muscle memory and mastery.

Exercise:

Consider purchasing a journal or notebook to capture the significant events that occur throughout your day. Feel free to use digital methods as well.

Experiment with selecting different times during the day to see what works best for you. Some of my clients place this notebook on their pillow to download their day and empty their minds before bed. Others place their journal on their office chair and reflect on the previous day before they begin the new one.

#251: "The key is to keep company only with people who uplift you, whose presence calls forth your best."

– Epictetus, classical Greek philosopher

When I engage a new client in a customized coaching relationship, we spend a considerable amount of time exploring their key personal and professional relationships. I often have them rate these relationships on a 1–10 scale to determine both the current level of support they provide as well as the importance they have for this individual moving forward.

Social support is as important to the coaching process as the client's own motivation and ability to pursue their goals.

Exercise:

Spend more time with those people who call forth your personal and professional best.

Spend less time with those people who are negative and critical.

Identify some people who uplift you and start spending time with them.

Finally, identify some of the most negative, judgmental people and stop spending time with them or giving them any "mindshare".

#252: "Dream big, but allow yourself the opportunity to start small and have your share of struggles in the beginning. The world's greatest composers weren't writing symphonies the day they first sat at the piano."

– Kevin O'Rourke, American running enthusiast

O'Rourke is suggesting that we consider our life as a splendid symphony and that we are all composers.

The other day, my wife Wendy downloaded a piano app onto her iPad and began to play around with it. She began with scales and made an effort at Chopsticks. She eventually wants to play the piano that was given to our family by her father many years ago.

Exercise:

What are a few of your big dreams and goals? What small steps must be taken, and what potential struggles must be faced, to help you develop the mastery to compose your personal and professional symphonies?

#253: "An eye for an eye will make the whole world blind."

– Mahatma Gandhi, Indian independence leader

I'm not a big fan of gossip, negativity, and conflict. For me, revenge is never sweet – and the idea of war is inconsistent with everything I hold dear.

When you look into the animal kingdom, you only see examples of killing as a means of eating and survival. Humans seems to have an appetite for conflict over the millenniums and today all you need to do is watch TV for the latest news report, sporting event, or reality TV show to see this.

Exercise:

How can you channel your inner Gandhi to make your own life, communities, and world more peaceful places?

#254: "We are betrayed by what is false within."

– George Meredith, Victorian poet and novelist

Imagine for a moment that your life has a soundtrack – an internal playlist that informs you about every aspect of your personal and professional life. What if, however, there was a poltergeist or some other form of gremlin that installed some of your playlist without your knowledge?

If this happens to be the case, you may find yourself dancing to or even singing a tune that could betray you.

Exercise:

Like trying on a piece of clothing when shopping, pay particular attention today and throughout this week to the ideas you express and the thoughts suggested by others, to see if they support or betray your very best self and true nature.

#255: "We know more than we know we know."

– Unknown

One of the coach's most powerful tools is the open-ended question: you know, those questions that can't be answered with a simple "yes" or "no".

Who could have imagined that the six simple trigger words: *who, what, when, where, why,* and *how* could bring forth a level of knowledge and wisdom in others far deeper than what we see on the surface?

Exercise:

Imagine yourself and others as an iceberg where what we know we know is only the observable part above the surface. (With icebergs, this is typically only one-eighth of the whole.)

Practice asking yourself and those around you more open-ended questions to discover how much more we actually know that lies below the surface.

#256: "Imagination is a quality given to man to compensate him for what he is not and a sense of humor was provided to console him for what he is."

– Oscar Wilde, Irish writer and poet

Self-awareness and the ability to adapt to life's circumstances are critical skills developed and enhanced during a coaching relationship.

Quite often, I discover many people I work with have strong "inner critics" and tend to emphasize their own perceived shortcomings. At the same time, many of these same individuals take themselves and life far too seriously, which often diminishes their pleasure and enjoyment of life.

Exercise:

Try on "Wilde coaching" by exercising both your imagination and sense of humor to bring greater fulfillment and satisfaction to your days.

Let your friends, mentors, and coaches know that you intend to make these efforts so that they can help you improve your likelihood of success.

#257: "You can rest assured that if you devote your time and attention to the highest advantage of others, the universe will support you."

– R. Buckminster Fuller, American architect and inventor

About two years ago, I picked up a copy of Dan Sullivan's book, *The Laws of Lifetime Growth*. Law #3 states that we should always make our contribution bigger than our reward.

Both Fuller and Sullivan suggest that focusing on creating new kinds of value for others expands our relationship with the outside world and somehow magically attracts new rewards and opportunities to us in return.

Exercise:

Imagine that giving to others and supporting their highest advantage is like making consistent daily bank deposits, and that these investments always have a high rate of return through the magic of compound interest.

#258: "Always bear in mind that your own resolution to succeed is more important than any [other] one thing."

– Abraham Lincoln, 16th American President

One of the questions I ask all of my coaching clients is, "What makes someone an excellent coach?"

People often include such attributes as:

- Superior listening skills
- Genuine caring
- Diversity of expertise and experience
- Optimism
- Integrity
- Commitment

Although all great qualities, this question – which happens to be a trick – has very little to do with the coach. The critical factor is "you": the person being coached.

As Lincoln points out, your resolution to succeed and willingness to do the work is paramount to achieving your goals.

Exercise:

Assess how strong your resolution is to pursue and achieve greater results in your personal and professional life. What added support do you require from within and from those around you to ensure your success?

#259: "The journey of a thousand miles begins and ends with one step."

– Lao Tzu, Chinese philosopher

We have all heard this famous quote a thousand times. What about all those steps in between?

Of course we would all acknowledge the importance of taking the initiative with the first step toward our goals. Once we have done so, we are at a new beginning point, ready to take the next first step.

In the beginning, it may be difficult to move toward our goals – however, with persistence and the development of this habit to act, we will be much more likely to find ourselves taking that last step to reach our desired destinations.

Exercise:

Identify at least one professional or personal goal that you deeply desire, where you find yourself procrastinating or simply stopped in your tracks.

Brainstorm alone or with others the first, second, etc., steps toward its achievement.

Before you know it, you will have arrived.

#260: "Choose yourself."

– Seth Godin, American author and entrepreneur

www.sethgodin.com

In recent months, I have met with numerous executives to explore next steps regarding their career advancement. Two of the most common options include advancement within their existing organization or creating an exit strategy to pursue greener pastures with another company.

Unfortunately in some cases, the entryway into the "C-suite" may be blocked, or the phone simply doesn't ring with those plum assignments. In some cases, even after considerable networking and outreach efforts, they have yet to be picked for the team.

Exercise:

Take out one of your business cards and turn it over to the blank side. Write your name then the title, "President", or a title of your choosing just under it.

By choosing yourself, you virtually eliminate all the current internal barriers that may be stopping you. Now all you need to do is overcome the external constraints to play your own game and make your ideal career a reality.

#261: "Discipline is the bridge between goals and accomplishment."

– Jim Rohn, American entrepreneur and motivational speaker

www.jimrohn.com

One of my core values is health, and one of my habits is daily exercise. The other day, I watched a special boot-camp session at my health club. In this session, the trainer and the participants created a supportive and highly disciplined environment to bridge the gap between each individual's current health and fitness status and their goals.

Exercise:

What areas of your professional or personal life are lacking the discipline needed to reach your goals?

Hire a coach (or drill sergeant) to support your efforts with a customized "boot-camp" to grow and strengthen your discipline muscle.

An alternative is to find a personal or professional partner and provide support for each other.

#262: "Don't fight forces: use them."

– R. Buckminster Fuller, American architect and inventor

As a former science teacher, I have always been interested in the forces of nature. Consider wind energy and wave energy, two forces of nature we often face in our outdoor activities.

If you happen to play golf, you know what it is like to drive a ball into 20 mile per hour headwind versus having the same breeze at your back.

In terms of water energy, have you ever tried to swim or row against the current or through an oncoming wave?

Exercise:

Explore the personal, professional, social, and cultural forces around you to see how you might use these energies versus fight against them to move forward in your life.

#263: "I learned that when I made people laugh, they liked me. This is a lesson I'll never forget."

– Art Buchwald, American humorist *(attrib.)*

While doing a bit of research on the subject of likeability, I came upon a list of attributes that include:

- Being honest

- Being humble

- Expressing empathy

- Being positive and optimistic

- Being polite

- Controlling anger and hostility

- Being a great listener

- And of course, having a great sense of humor

By demonstrating your sense of humor, you show a playfulness and happiness that attract others toward you.

Exercise:

Check out your humor level and restock it if necessary. Consider humor websites, joke books, or even ask your friends and family for their best stuff.

Spreading a few more smiles around definitely pays off.

#264: "Try something different, try something new; you might find it likes you and you like it too!"

– Dr. Seuss, American children's author

How open are you to doing things in new and different ways? How frequently do you operate from the relative safety of your comfort zone? What are the benefits of trying something new?

Today I had an extremely engaging coaching session with one of my clients. This young man is one of the smartest, most creative people in his organization, and boy, does he think differently!

I asked him, "How will your company make money in the future, and what new initiatives will have it remain relevant and a leader in its field?"

To make a long story short, he developed a template for a project to reinvent how the company currently operates, to potentially save the organization over a million dollars.

Exercise:

Consider taking a new and different action today in both your personal and professional life. Use the following sentences as a guide to help you try something new:

In _____ situation I usually do _____.

Instead, I am going to try _____.

#265: "Great minds like a think."

– The Economist

www.economist.com

If I were predictable, I might have used the quote, "Great minds think alike" – but how interesting would that be?

Did you know that based on research from the Jenkins Group, a third of high school students who graduate never read another book for the rest of their lives? 42% of college graduates never read another book after college, and 80% of families did not buy or read a book last year.

Great minds, like great bodies, need exercise. Reading and thinking about new ideas is like doing cerebral sit-ups, toning our cores to have those six-pack abs we desire.

Exercise:

How will you exercise your mental muscles in the coming days, weeks, and years ahead to avoid the atrophy of the mind?

Consider taking the "use it or lose it" mental fitness challenge in Episode 10 of Brain Games, from National Geographic:

braingames.nationalgeographic.com/episode/10

#266: "How do I work? I grope."

– Albert Einstein, German-American theoretical physicist

How about that? A man many consider synonymous with the term "genius" admits to pursuing his work in a non-linear and haphazard way.

Perhaps this groping was part of his genius. Maybe square pegs and round holes can fit in some way if we simply grope around to take more frequent quantum leaps in how we solve problems.

Exercise:

Select an issue or challenge you are currently facing and set up a "groping" session instead of a general brainstorming session.

Play with possibilities as if you were from another world where playfulness, novelty, and experimentation were the only objectives.

#267: "How am I doing?"

– Ed Koch, American lawyer and politician

Ed Koch, the former mayor of New York City, who passed away in February 2013, was well known for the quote above. This short question is perhaps the quickest and simplest possible example of a performance appraisal.

During their careers, many business professionals experience a wide variety of feedback vehicles, including the famous 360° feedback tool that can approach 100 pages in length. Who has that much extra time these days?

Koch used his simple question to ask the citizens of New York for feedback so he could make appropriate adjustments to his leadership to improve his performance and hopefully serve his constituents better.

Exercise:

Consider asking this question of those closest to you in your personal and professional life as it relates to the numerous roles you play.

Take their coaching and adjust your approaches, looking for what works to your and other people's advantage.

#268: "When you're presented with the opportunity to improve someone's life, to help them go through a particularly difficult challenge, to engage with great comrades and achieve a noble mission – what could be luckier?"

– Unknown cadet, quoted by Jim Collins, business consultant and author

This quote is a call to action. It is a call for you to channel your inner coach. It's a call to help those around you realize their most cherished goals, or simply navigate their worlds a bit more smoothly.

To begin with, view this supportive process as a personal scavenger hunt in which these individuals already have the answers or resources they require within them.

Should you discover that what they need is not within arm's length, please do help them find the missing pieces outside of themselves. These may well include what you can bring to the situation.

Exercise:

Select one person in your personal or professional world to help achieve their most noble mission. They will be lucky to have your support and I bet you will feel lucky too.

#269: "Only dead fish swim with the stream all the time."

– Linda Ellerbee, American journalist

We have all heard phrases such as, "Go with the flow", and "Take the path of least resistance", as ways to simply and effortlessly navigate life. When we take such advice, we are almost always carried along by factors not influenced or controlled by us, and we wind up somewhere we didn't intend.

When we chart our own course and swim against the current, we strengthen our ability to navigate our own life's journey and realize our deepest held desires.

Exercise:

Where in your personal and professional life are you being carried downstream by someone else's current?

What goals have you come alive, so that you use your fins to swim upstream and realize your vision?

#270: "A man who works with his hands is a laborer; a man who works with his hands and his brain is a craftsman; but a man who works with his hands and his brain and his heart is an artist."

– Louis Nizer, American trial lawyer

What percent of your day do you function as a laborer, a craftsman, or an artist?

Consider which of these roles bring you the greatest satisfaction and fulfillment.

Exercise:

Make a definite choice to reduce those roles that diminish your joy and increase those areas that provide the most.

Share this insight with family members, co-workers, mentors, or a coach that could support your intention.

#271: "A prudent question is one-half of wisdom."

– Francis Bacon, English philosopher

One crucial tool for most coaches, including myself, is the question. Below are some of my favorites:

1. What results in life are essential for you to see yourself as a success?

2. What qualities do you hope to expand or develop to be your best future self?

3. What would you like people to say about you at the end of your life?

4. What inspires you?

5. What are you passionate about?

6. And of course ... what else?

Exercise:

To reap the other half of wisdom, answer at least one of these questions today and others over the course of the coming week.

Share this exercise and your answers with those you care about in your personal and professional life.

Coach and support one another in living life each day consistently with your answers.

#272: "One thought driven home is better than three left on base."

– James Liter, writer

It's hard not to be a baseball fan if you live in the Detroit area. We love our Tigers. In years past, when the team did not quite have it all together, they stranded many a base runner. Today's team seems to have a greater confidence and the capacity to bring those runners home.

In a world of business, this quote from James Liter suggests that our ideas and creative solutions may be like these baseball runners – and we often leave them stranded.

Exercise:

Select at least one professional or personal idea, objective or goal that you simply must bring home.

Create a compelling, enthralling vision of this idea so you can get "buy-in" from your community. Work with them to achieve it together, celebrating your collective hard work along the way.

#273: "A smile is a curve that sets everything straight."

– Phyllis Diller, American comedian

From my research on the importance of smiling, here are a few interesting facts I'd like to share:

Smiling:

- Slows the heart rate and relaxes the body

- Releases endorphins, diminishes stress, and improves our mood

- Must have been used by the Seven Dwarves to increase their productivity as they whistled while they worked

- Improves relationships by increasing trust and building empathy

- Makes us more appealing and attractive – yes, smiling makes us look younger

- Improves our immune system and lowers our blood pressure

- Conveys optimism and positivity that helps us be more successful

Exercise:

How can you smile more and turn that frown upside down to improve your life and, as Phyllis Diller suggests, set everything straight?

#274: "I not only use the brains I have, I use all the brains I can borrow."

– Calvin Coolidge, 30th American President

We have all heard the phrase, "Two heads are better than one." Research on this subject demonstrates this is generally true where there is a high degree of openness and communication regarding individual perspective and points of view.

However, in cases where this openness and collaborative communication is missing, or suboptimal, more brains can actually produce worse results.

Exercise:

Consider picking up a copy of Edward de Bono's book, *Six Thinking Hats*, to support both your own individual and group thinking.

This is a great example of putting on your thinking cap (or hat).

#275: "There's no greater power than to be in harmony with oneself."

– Panache Desai, American spiritual writer

Do you like music? Me too. Great music has the power to move all of us. Think of some of your favorite songs, along with those smooth and often catchy melodies. I bet you could hum or sing some of them.

The action of tuning an instrument demonstrates that there is a certain frequency of vibration that resonates perfectly to make it sound just right.

Exercise:

Imagine you are a special and unique instrument of God that resonates at a particular frequency based on your unique abilities, gifts, values, and beliefs.

Your job today is to "take note" of this special tune and play away.

#276: "If a man does his best, what else is there?"

– George S. Patton, American general

We live in a highly competitive society. Winning seems to be all that counts in so many areas of our lives. Just look at sports, business, and even politics. However, if we examine how often any one individual or organization wins, we are often surprised at the modest or even low percentages.

This pursuit of winning and the pursuit of the perfect outcome unfortunately leaves far too many of us falling short, often with negative views of ourselves and others.

Exercise:

Be your best self today and all this week, and use that as the only standard you measure yourself against.

Don't be surprised by how great you feel – and by the considerable results you produce.

#277: "An investment in knowledge pays the best interest."

– Benjamin Franklin, diplomat, inventor, and Founding Father of the United States

The people who know me best know how much I love to learn. Learning is part of my fundamental fabric and is one of my signature strengths. Perhaps that is why, over 20 years ago, I was so attracted to the profession of coaching, where personal and professional growth and development is a top priority.

Not only do I enjoy learning new things each and every day, I find sharing this learning and supporting others on their own growth journey amazingly satisfying.

Exercise:

Select one or two things you would like to learn about today. Ask others around you to teach you things – or simply tap into the web.

Share what you learn with others in your world to compound your interest.

#278: "Every human has four endowments – self-awareness, conscience, independent will, and creative imagination. These give us the ultimate human freedom ... The power to choose, to respond, to change."

– Stephen Covey, American self-help author

In 2012, we all lost a legend in the personal development world in Stephen Covey. Among his many accomplishments, he was recognized as one of Time Magazine's "25 Most Influential Americans."

He dedicated his life to demonstrating how every person can truly control and influence their own destiny – and the quote above sums it up pretty well.

Exercise:

How are you currently doing in your personal mastery journey to improve your self-awareness, conscience, independent will, and creative imagination, to maximize your power to choose, respond, and change?

What can you do to expand these capacities even further?

#279: "To do what you love and feel it matters; how could anything be more fun?"

– Katharine Graham, American publisher

Many coaches share a common mission and purpose: to assist and support others in living their best life.

Fundamental to this mission is its expression in our vocations and professional worlds. In the words of another quote, "If you love what you do, you will never work a day in your life."

Connecting *who you are* with *what you do* is critical for all of us if we are to be happy and fully expressed as individuals.

Exercise:

To move yourself forward in this area, I suggest you do both a values clarification assessment and a signature strength appraisal. By blending the results of these exercises, you will see the route that can be taken to fulfill your professional destiny.

You can use the values clarification assessment from Quote #27 and you can do a signature strength appraisal based on the book, *Now Discover Your Strengths*, by Marcus Buckingham.

#280: "To seduce almost anyone, ask for and listen to his opinion."

– Malcolm Forbes, American publisher

When I conduct my individual and organizational personal excellence workshops, a key tool I share with participants is the Communications Toolbox. This includes six simple techniques that emphasize the importance of demonstrating sincere interest and truly listening to others.

Others' thoughts, ideas, and opinions on any subject happen to be the key to unlock our ability to influence them. This ability to tune into others' fundamental human frequency is like finding a perfectly tailored pair of gloves that fit our hands just right.

Exercise:

Email me at barry@dempcoaching.com with "Communication Toolbox" in the subject line, and I will send you a copy.

Two books that I find useful on this subject are:

- *Fierce Conversations*, by Susan Scott

- *Crucial Conversations*, by Kerry Patterson and others

#281: "When it comes to life, the critical thing is whether you take things for granted, or take them with gratitude."

– G.K. Chesterton, English novelist

After my mother Rose passed away in 2012, we had the great privilege to have my father Marvin living with us. I must admit I was a bit concerned how it would change our lives, since not too long ago, Wendy and I became empty nesters.

At the age of 87, my father does not move as fast, and this has caused me to become far more aware of and self-reflective about my own life. I am pleased to say that with his wisdom and influence, I am taking far more things with gratitude than for granted.

Exercise:

Use today to slow down to half speed and look around at all the wonderful things that make up your life.

Go out of your way to thank those who are on this journey with you and consider sharing your insights about this exercise.

#282: "There can be no joy in living without joy in work."

– St. Thomas Aquinas, Italian Dominican friar and priest

My brother Neal is an outstanding child psychiatrist who lives on the East Coast. The last couple of years have been quite difficult for him due to his lack of enjoyment in his work, caused by a dramatic change in his organization's management.

His level of responsibility is high, and he is compensated quite well, but this level of reward makes virtually no difference to his level of satisfaction.

I'm proud to say that he just accepted a new (and likely more satisfying) job with a bit less pay to once again hopefully find joy in this very important part of life.

Exercise:

How can you contribute to and expand your satisfaction and enjoyment at work?

If that's improbable or impossible, how can you make the courageous change required in order to find joy in your working life?

#283: "Words are small shapes in the gorgeous chaos of the world. They bring the world into focus; they corral ideas; they hone thoughts; they paint watercolors of perception."

– Diane Ackerman, American author

www.dianeackerman.com

When I was growing up, one of the most popular board games was Scrabble. This game brought families and friends together to test our abilities to take those small shapes and find focus from initial chaos.

Today, the number of popular word games is staggering, with some of the most popular being: Words with Friends, Wheel of Fortune, Bookworm, Boggle, and the ever-popular crossword puzzle.

Exercise:

To build up your word-power muscle, keep an old-fashioned dictionary or thesaurus handy to review daily when you identify a word you don't know, or when you are writing.

Alternatively, check out:

www.dictionary.reference.com/wordoftheday

or a similar site or app.

#284: "An apple a day keeps the doctor away."

– Proverbial

The other day while I was at my health club, I noticed one of the personal trainers eating an apple. Perhaps because I have quotes on my mind all the time, I found myself saying this familiar phrase.

When I got to my office that day – after eating my daily apple – I decided to do a bit of research on this and found out that:

- Apples are filled with five grams of soluble fiber that has been shown to reduce intestinal disorders such as diverticulitis and possibly some forms of cancer.

- They contain pectin which can help to reduce cholesterol levels by lowering insulin secretions.

- They can lower the risk of respiratory diseases such as asthma if eaten regularly.

- They're low in calories and packed with vitamins A, C, flavonoids, and as many as 12,000 other phytonutrients to support good health.

- Apple cider vinegar has been shown to prevent the formation of kidney stones.

Exercise:

Consider going to your local market or specialty grocer, and go on an apple safari. Select at least five and perhaps up to a dozen different varieties, and do a taste test to see which you prefer.

Some of my favorites are Honeycrisp, Jazz, Fuji, Pink Lady, Granny Smith, Gala, Empire, and Northern Spy.

#285: "Problems are in your life so that you can discover potentials that you didn't even know you had."

– Barry Michels, American self-help author

What exactly is a problem? We might describe it as a "source of perplexity, distress, or difficulty." What is it that makes some issues a problem for some of us and not for others?

Perhaps some people who navigate their worlds with greater ease have simply addressed such matters and realized the potential within themselves to handle them.

Exercise:

Instead of looking at your professional and personal problems as "bad" and something to avoid, see each one in a new light as an opportunity to learn and grow.

Choose a problem you're currently facing, and visit it in a new or different way to solve it.

#286: "The world has a habit of making room for the man whose words and actions show that he knows where he is going."

– Napoleon Hill, American self-help author

Self-confidence can be a slippery slope. When we have too little, we are often paralyzed. If we demonstrate too much, we could be perceived as cocky, arrogant, or closed-minded.

Exercise:

Three strategies to develop and enhance your confidence without going too far include:

1. Working on critical skills and abilities through committed and consistent practice to enhance your competency

2. Working on your ability to remain calm and centered when faced with events that can trigger upsets and strong emotions

3. Speaking and acting each day in ways consistent with your core values and fundamental beliefs – they will provide you with both direction and personal power to step confidently through your world

#287: "The optimist already sees the scar over the wound; the pessimist sees the wound underneath the scar."

– Ernst Schroder, German mathematician

The war between optimists and pessimists has been raging for longer than anyone can remember. Which camp are you in? For the purpose of this quote, please don't take the back door and choose "realist" – though I do appreciate you thinking outside the box.

It turns out that both strategies come in pretty handy, depending on the situation. Optimists tend to have a focus on growth and advancement. Pessimists, on the other hand, tend to be more focused on security and safety. Schroeder was probably an optimist, given the fact that a scar is a protective and healing phenomenon supporting new growth.

Exercise:

Consider answering the following questions:

Where are you engaged in the rapid healing and growth from wounds you may recently have experienced?

Where are you still feeling the wounds of the past that should have fully healed by now?

What are you going to do to bring about healing? Who will you ask to help?

#288: "Instead of seeking new landscapes, develop new eyes."

– Marcel Proust, French novelist

The capacity to perceive things is perhaps one of the most important aspects of coaching. The current paradigms and mental models that we have developed over the course of our lives both serve and limit us at the same time. Our eyes are the proverbial lenses through which we view the world around us.

Just as a pair of sunglasses modifies the intensity of light on a sunny day, our willingness to view things in a new light creates the opportunity for new and more useful perspectives to emerge.

Exercise:

Imagine that you've just returned from laser surgery or a cataract procedure. The surgeon has given you two new eyes that not only have you see more clearly but also enhance your capacity of seeing opportunities and beauty.

Now imagine those eyes can also enhance your creativity, innovation, positivity, gratitude, and overall happiness.

#289: "We should learn from the mistakes of others. We don't have time to make them all ourselves."

– Groucho Marx, American comedian

A few weeks ago, I was watching a video interview of Rich Roll by Jonathan Fields as part of his Good Life Project. Roll is a top Ultraman competitor who is considered one of the fittest men in the world.

It wasn't always this way. In fact, earlier in his life, Roll was a drug addict and alcoholic. Through his own story and miraculous turn around, he has inspired thousands of people to pursue greater health and vitality through dramatic dietary changes and intensive exercise.

Exercise:

Examine the lives of people you know personally and professionally to see what lessons you could use to live a more fulfilling life yourself. What positive behaviors will you emulate and which mistakes will you definitely avoid?

#290: "Action conquers fear."

– Peter Nivio Zarlenga, author

Over the next day or two, take particular notice of people who are experiencing worry or outright fear – especially if one of those people is you. One thing I bet you notice is the degree of paralysis, procrastination, and inactivity associated with this emotion.

Terms like: *crippled, frozen, riddled,* and *stuck* all point to this debilitating condition.

Simply the act of moving one step at a time helps to break these bonds and frees us once again to move our worlds forward.

Exercise:

Whenever you are experiencing fear, share how you're feeling with someone immediately, and seek their support to act quickly before the cement of this crippling emotion has a chance to dry.

#291: "It is not a daily increase but a daily decrease. Hack away at the inessentials."

– Bruce Lee, Chinese American martial artist and actor

When I speak with the majority of my clients and ask them how they are, they almost always say something that includes words such as: *busy, swamped, overwhelmed,* or *slammed.*

Most of us are faced with increasingly complex lives. Unfortunately, spending time, space, and energy on the inessentials can be exhausting. Bruce Lee suggests here that we can take particular note of what can be eliminated from our lives, to reclaim fulfillment, vitality, and happiness.

Exercise:

Explore the following categories as you look to decrease or perhaps eliminate things from your life:

- Clutter
- Subscriptions
- Email
- Clothing
- Toxic relationships
- Technology

#292: "If an egg is broken by outside force, life ends. If broken by inside force, life begins. Great things always begin from inside."

– Jim Kwik, American learning expert

www.jimkwik.com

In many ways, the coaching process can be compared to helping individuals (or organizations) come out of their shells.

Just as a bird forces itself to emerge from its shell, the coaching process, with its powerful questions, taps into the power of people's commitments to help them break free of the confines of their own limits.

Exercise:

Select one area of your life today where you plan to break out of your current constraints, to spread your wings and fly. Secure the assistance of a friend, family member, colleague, or coach to support you in this effort.

#293: "I am seeking, I am striving, I am in it with all my heart."

– Vincent van Gogh, Dutch painter

The other night, I was watching a show about Mars and the current plans to send a manned mission there by the year 2033. The complexity and enormity of this undertaking was inspiring.

I guess it is within our very nature as humans to seek and strive for new levels of knowledge, adventure, and accomplishment – and yet, some of us slow down and even stop in these efforts. We sometimes find ourselves in dead-end jobs, dead-end relationships, and general life ruts where we feel stuck or trapped.

Exercise:

Complete the following statement:

I am looking forward to _____.

Keep asking yourself, "What else? What else? What else?" with all your heart, until you revive the seeker and striver in you.

#294: "I believe in getting into hot water. It keeps you clean."

– G.K. Chesterton, English novelist

Do you ever feel like one day seems to run into the next, where things seem to be a bit dull or routine? Perhaps we can do as G.K. Chesterton suggests and rinse off the dirt and freshen up a bit ... even if that means risking something new.

I know I feel much better when I splash a bit of water on my face to renew myself for what's next to come in my day.

Exercise:

What areas of hot water can you get yourself into today to brighten up your world?

(You may need to risk not agreeing with others and not fitting in!)

#295: "A lesson taught with humor is a lesson retained."

– Ruth K. Westheimer, aka "Dr. Ruth", American sex therapist

One of the primary reasons I chose to pursue the profession of coaching, over 20 years ago, was because of the considerable shortcomings of other forms of training and development. We all have books, binders, tapes, and seminar folders sitting on our shelves that are barely remembered, and collecting dust.

Coaching is all about stickiness and sustainability, where the lessons learned in an experiential way, stay with us and often become habituated.

Humor, as Westheimer suggests, is a great way to make an idea or experience memorable, sticky, and sustainable.

Exercise:

Where can you add a bit – or a bunch – of humor and fun to lessons being shared in both your professional and personal worlds?

Consider Googling, "The use of humor to support learning", and see what you discover.

#296: "A man travels the world over in search of what he needs and returns home to find it."

– George Moore, Irish novelist

One of my favorite movies from my youth was *The Wizard of Oz*. Back then, it was only on once a year – and on that day, we actually got to eat dinner in our living room on those corny folding trays.

The fundamental message of the film was, "There's no place like home", which fits perfectly with Moore's quote.

Exercise:

Today and this week, explore those things that you are searching for and see just how many are in your own home or community.

#297: "Constant kindness can accomplish much. As the sun makes ice melt, kindness causes misunderstanding, mistrust, and hostility to evaporate."

– Albert Schweitzer, German / French humanitarian

Here in Michigan, we are preparing for the upcoming winter. The leaves are changing color and starting to fall, and our mornings are beginning to get crisp and cool.

I personally like the idea of kindness as a proverbial defroster that we can use whenever we wish to bring greater warmth into our worlds.

Exercise:

Where (and to whom) can you extend greater kindness today, to increase your capacity to accomplish much?

#298: "A true friend never gets in your way unless you happen to be going down."

– Arnold H. Glasow, American author

Do you know who your true friends are? The quote above by Glasow is a pretty good test to help you identify the best ones. They are the people who support us in living our best lives and stand for us being all we can be.

At the same time, they are the people who are there during life's challenging and difficult times to lend us a shoulder to lean on – or carry us completely when things are at their darkest.

Exercise:

Thank the friends around you for being there in both good and difficult times, and while doing so, look within yourself to see how you stack up as a friend to others.

#299: "The best thing about the future is that it comes one day at a time."

– Abraham Lincoln, 16th American President

One of my philosophies of life is that what we do each day and who we do it with determines our satisfaction in the moment and manifests our future.

Consider yourself as a gardener, where each day you sow the seeds of success in your professional and personal world, and take care to water and weed your crop throughout the growing season to reap the harvest of a better future.

Exercise:

Take particular note of the daily behaviors and habits that are contributing to a better future.

Recognize where some of your daily efforts or lack of action are creating a less than desirable future and know that it's not too late to start over tomorrow – because the future, as Lincoln suggests, comes one day at a time.

#300: "The great thing in this world is not so much where we stand as in what direction we are moving."

– Oliver Wendell Holmes, Sr., American physician and author

Imagine that you have decided to climb Mount Everest. Consider all the plans and activities required for you to achieve what only 1,500 or so people have ever done.

The amount of time that people actually stand on the summit is just a fraction of the time spent going from base camp to the top ... and that's not even counting all the training and preparation time.

Exercise:

Examine your own level of fulfillment in the journeys you have undertaken and are currently on, to realize it's the direction and the process of living each day that holds much of the sweetness of life.

#301: "Optimism is the faith that leads to achievement. Nothing can be done without hope and confidence."

– Helen Keller, deaf-blind American author and activist

One of the factors most associated with success in a coaching relationship is optimism. Perhaps one reason for this is that optimists see setbacks as temporary and find the courage and tenacity to stay the course toward their goals. Pessimists, on the other hand, tend to see setbacks and failures as more permanent, and often give up far too soon with, "What's the use?" or "It's far too difficult."

Keller was faced with major life obstacles: she was deaf and blind from the age of 19 months. She became the first deaf-blind person to graduate with a Bachelor of Arts degree. She was also an activist for women's suffrage and workers' rights, and many other progressive causes. She even published 12 books during her lifetime.

Exercise:

To exercise your optimism muscle, consider one of the following books:

Learned Optimism and *Authentic Happiness*, both by Martin Seligman

Happier by Tal Ben-Shahar (a well-known professor at Harvard)

#302: "The price of anything is the amount of life you exchange for it."

– Henry David Thoreau, American author and philosopher

One of my favorite quotes in this book is, "Time is the coin of your life." How we spend our time and who we spend it with literally has a price.

Exercise:

Examine your life domains and ask yourself if each investment of your valuable life equity was worth it.

Consider making a few adjustments by doing more of some things, less of others, and starting a few new and interesting activities – and of course stopping those intolerable ones that you regret the most.

#303: "We forfeit three-quarters of ourselves in order to be like other people."

– Arthur Schopenhauer, German philosopher

If this quote has some truth in it, is it such a bad thing?

What if you were to take all the greatest qualities of people you most admire to create this initial three-quarters of yourself? Not bad, huh? The last quarter gets to be a completely manifested part of yourself – unencumbered by anything external.

If you add this all together, I'd say you'd have a pretty remarkable you!

Exercise:

Look at yourself today and begin piecing together the "future you" from those remarkable people around you, as well as through the development of your own unique gifts and talents.

#304: "Lighthouses don't go running all over an island looking for boats to save; they just stand there shining."

– Anne Lamott, American writer

www.facebook.com/AnneLamott

My coaching business is a bit unusual in that I hold most of my sessions in person, in my office. Instead of running all over town to meet with each individual client, I created a secure harbor for these coaching sessions, in a calm and confidential location, removed from the often hectic rushing around that comprises many people's days.

Exercise:

Where are you currently running all over your personal and professional "island" looking for boats to save?

How could you let your own shining light act as a beacon to bring greater sanity, security, and success into your world?

#305: "Our business in life is not to get ahead of others but to get ahead of ourselves, to break our own records, to outstrip our yesterday by outperforming today."

– Stewart B. Johnson, British artist

One of the key concepts I use in my work as a coach is "creative tension". I came across this term in Robert Fritz's book, *The Path of Least Resistance*, published in 1989. It points to the power of a better future to literally pull us from our current realities, to act each day to make that future a reality.

In the case of Johnson's quote, we have the opportunity to become better than ourselves in any areas we wish.

Exercise:

Select one area in your personal or professional life where you wish to outperform your current self. Develop a project action plan with a coach, colleague, friend, mentor, or family member to help you break your own records and outstrip your yesterdays.

#306: "The heart should be cultivated with more assiduity than the head."

– Noah Webster, American lexicographer

Noah Webster registered the copyright on his American dictionary of the English language (*A Compendious Dictionary of the English Language*) over 185 years ago.

When I was young, I was not such an avid reader. Words – especially words like "assiduity" – tripped me up, due to my lack of understanding and my impatience.

Both of my parents installed the discipline of taking time to learn the meaning of such words, much to my initial frustration. Today, I know it was the assiduity of their hearts that had me persist in this flagging effort, to help me learn and grow.

Exercise:

Imagine what life would be like if Webster had also created a dictionary of the heart. What other books and resources – such as the Bible, Torah, Koran, or works of literature – provide such heart-developing wisdom? Perhaps a dose of assiduity is called for here.

#307: "Don't compromise yourself. You're all you've got."

– Janis Joplin, American singer-songwriter

In November 2013, our family and friends celebrated the wedding of my daughter Rachel in Sanibel Island, Florida. It was simply the best event I've ever attended. The ceremony was on a secluded beach, with the added bonus of a beautiful rainbow, an inspiring sunset, and even some dolphins swimming by.

Videographers, photographers, great food, a beautiful reception, and dancing till midnight were just some of the other things that made it special.

The credit for these memories goes to many people, especially my extraordinary wife, Wendy, and my beautiful daughter for never compromising their vision of a fairytale wedding come true.

Exercise:

What could you achieve by not compromising? How can you take a step closer to your highest vision today?

#308: "Character is revealed by action, action is motivated by character."

– Norton Wright

There is an organization called the Josephson Institute that teaches "Six Pillars of Character" in its youth educational programs. These pillars are:

1. **Trustworthiness** – being honest, being reliable, and doing what you say you'll do

2. **Respect** – following the Golden Rule

3. **Responsibility** – being accountable, doing your best, and setting a good example

4. **Fairness** – playing by the rules, being open-minded, taking turns, and sharing

5. **Caring** – being kind, compassionate, forgiving, and showing gratitude

6. **Citizenship** – getting involved in your communities to make them better, protecting the environment, and volunteering

Exercise:

How will you be motivated by and act consistently with these six pillars?

How can you coach, mentor, and support those around you – especially children – to develop these qualities through your example?

#309: "People often say that motivation doesn't last. Well, neither does bathing. That's why we recommend it daily."

– Zig Ziglar, American motivational speaker

There are many things we do on a daily basis to live our lives to the fullest. That means eating healthy foods, exercising our bodies, getting sufficient sleep, working on our relationships, engaging in meaningful work, and of course, bathing!

I'd like to suggest that, in addition to taking our usual vitamin supplements, we get an extra dose of vitamin "M" – Motivation – to help us be our very best.

Exercise:

Select and use a variety of motivational resources – such as empowering books, CDs, videos, and of course powerful quotes – on a daily basis, to keep you fully engaged and to keep your attitude in top condition.

Select at least one motivating idea or concept and share it with others in your personal and professional life to enhance their days.

#310: "I keep six honest serving-men (They taught me all I knew); Their names are What and Why and When and How and Where and Who."

– Robert Louis Stevenson, Scottish novelist and poet

Perhaps the most profound and impactful resource in the coach's toolbox is the open-ended question. Beginning a question with one of the "six serving-men" above opens up the doors of knowledge and wisdom, if we take the time to master them.

As an added bonus, these questions also open up doors to more satisfying and fulfilling relationships in our professional and personal lives.

Exercise:

Consider visiting my website at www.dempcoaching.com and download a copy of my workbook on Masterful Relationships from:

www.dempcoaching.com/download-your-free-workbooks

The password is **barrydemp** (all lower-case). This also gives you access to my other two workbooks – enjoy!

If you have difficultly downloading the workbook, please email me at barry@dempcoaching.com with the words "Masterful Relationships" in the subject line and I will send you a copy.

#311: "There are two types of people in this world: those who walk into a room and say, 'There you are!' and those who say, 'Here I am!'"

– Unknown

A cornerstone to personal excellence and personal effectiveness is the ability to develop and sustain effective relationships.

Previously, we have reviewed a wide variety of tools and techniques to do just that. Fundamental to those tools is taking a sincere *interest* in others, showing our interest in their favorite subject – themselves.

On the other hand, when we focus on being *interesting*, we often come across as egotistical and self-centered, which repels others.

Exercise:

Ask for some feedback or coaching from those close to you and determine how much of a "There you are" versus "Here I am" person you are.

If the feedback you receive does not match up with what you desire, place a reminder card in your home and workplace with, "Be interested versus interesting" on it.

#312: "All words are pegs to hang ideas on."

– Henry Ward Beecher, American clergyman and social reformer

A close friend of mine named Allen, who unfortunately passed away too soon, was a very handy person. He could fix almost anything and he had a wide variety of tools to fit almost any need.

His garage was a veritable "Home Depot" with an immaculate collection displayed in the most organized manner. Included in his collection was a peg board with hooks that accepted each specific tool – with, you guessed it, an outline of the tool to show the user where to hang it when the job was done.

Exercise:

Pay particular attention today to the words you and others are using to create your world. Determine the extent to which the ideas that are generated build something wonderful, or in some cases, take things apart.

#313: "There's only one corner of the universe you can be certain of improving, and that's your own self."

- Aldous Huxley, English author

In my first career, over 30 years ago, I was a science teacher. Two subjects I found most fascinating were astronomy and physics.

Entropy is constantly at work expanding the universe and bringing disorder to our world. Fortunately, as Huxley suggests, we can use our own energies to counter this disorder and design the world as we desire.

Exercise:

How will you use your energy today to improve your corner of the universe?

How can you combine your energies with others to make even larger improvements in your world?

#314: "What we see when watching others depends on the clarity of the window through which we look."

– Unknown

Driving in Michigan, specifically in the Detroit metropolitan area, is challenging for numerous reasons. If we eliminate poor roads, construction, and heavy traffic, we are left with what I call visibility challenges. Rain, fog, road salt, frost, snow, and splattered insects all have a way of reducing the clarity of our windshields.

I dislike not having clarity so much that I just had a special window treatment applied to our new SUV to better help us see where we are going.

Exercise:

What are some of your obstructing views, beliefs, and attitudes about others that are blocking your clear and objective view?

How can you apply your own perceptional "Windex" to help clarify what you see in others and in yourself?

#315: "A good head and a good heart are always a formidable combination."

– Nelson Mandela, South African anti-apartheid President

I am sitting in a hotel room outside Lansing, Michigan. It is early morning and I am waiting to begin my day by attending a regional coaching meeting where I will make my best effort to expand my mind, to forward my skills as a coach.

Beyond this mind-expanding effort is the realization that I sincerely enjoy being part of a community of fellow coaches. They have hearts filled with love and the generous desire to use their vocation to make their world and the worlds of others a better place.

Exercise:

What effort are you making (and what effort can you make) to strengthen and expand your own head and heart combo, in order to better your world?

#316: "The race will go to the curious, the slightly mad, and those with an unsatiated passion for learning and dare-deviltry."

– Tom Peters, American business author

A few weekends ago, I went to see the Formula 1 racing movie *Rush,* directed by Ron Howard. In this true story of the rivalry between two top drivers, from the 70s, was a healthy dose of passion, slight madness, and dare-deviltry which actually helped these two individuals win many races.

I would almost never describe myself this way: I rarely exceed the speed limit! On the other hand, what I lack in dare-deviltry, I think I make up for in curiosity and passion for learning and achievement.

Exercise:

What races are you trying to win in your professional and personal life?

How can you mobilize your curiosity, passion, and dare-deviltry to see many checkered flags in the future?

#317: "Habit is the daily battle-ground of character."

– Dan Coats, American Senator

www.coats.senate.gov

Many of us engage in a variety of not-so-wonderful habits that could be called "character flaws". These habits include eating junk food, not exercising, and spending money we don't have, leaving us in debt.

On the other hand, the good and noble habits that demonstrate character often occur initially as a battle-ground, due to the need to go outside our comfort zones.

Most people of high character would suggest that the rewards of these habits are well worth it – and over time they become far less of a struggle to maintain.

Exercise:

Choose one of your current undesirable habits and promise yourself (and those around you) that you will replace it with one that demonstrates your highest character.

If you would like additional help with this and other habits you may wish to develop, consider purchasing and implementing the strategies in Charles Duhigg's book, *The Power of Habit*.

#318: "People will cling to an unsatisfactory way of life rather than change in order to get something better, for fear of getting something worse."

– Eric Hoffer, American philosopher

Do you know any living examples of the definition of insanity? You know, those people who keep on doing the same thing over and over, yet they expect a different result.

Perhaps one reason for their stuckness is what Hoffer suggests: the fear of getting a worse result if they change their ways.

What I have found in my years of coaching and in my own life is that high levels of commitment, combined with multiple levels of support over extended periods of time, almost always produce far better results.

Exercise:

To support you in altering some unsatisfactory part of your life, try this three-step exercise.

1. Identify your top commitments in your life that you wish to realize.

2. Rally support from all parts of your world.

3. Stay in action toward these objectives and accept the risk, and over time your life will be improved.

Repeat as often as you wish.

#319: "The gratification comes in the doing, not in the result."

– James Dean, American actor

My son, Dan, is a very special person for many reasons. From the time he was a little boy, he was always fascinated by many forms of mechanical and computer related activities. Dan would lose himself in the process of building things with K'nex, Legos, and various other objects or building kits.

He even wrote, illustrated, and self-published his first animal book at age 5. In high school, Dan participated in the robotic club and in college, he was a member of the programming and video game design club, where he would sometimes work 48 hours straight over a weekend to help create a new game.

Today, Dan is a top computer programmer working for one of the most respected health care software development firms in the world.

His vocational and even some avocational software design and programming efforts bring Dan great gratification in the "doing". This has been and continues to be his passion.

Exercise:

What vocational and avocational activities bring you the greatest gratification and satisfaction in the "doing", not simply in the result?

How can you do even more of these activities to enhance your professional and personal life?

#320: "If you can't explain it to a six year old, you don't understand it yourself."

– Albert Einstein, theoretical physicist

In the world of physics, perhaps no one is more famous than Einstein. He is best known for the formula $E=mc^2$ where E is energy, m stands for mass, and c represents the speed of light.

There is genius in simplicity, in that it brings ideas and insight into our lives. Compare programming your first VCR with the simplicity of many of our plug-and-play devices today.

Exercise:

Look up "Occam's Razor" and explore how making things in your life far simpler is a road toward unleashing your own genius and creating a more user-friendly, workable world.

#321: "Dreams are powerful reflections of your actual growth potential."

– Denis Waitley and Reni L. Witt, American authors

www.waitley.com

The vast majority of individuals who work with a coach have "personal growth and development" as a core value. They're constantly engaged in challenging themselves (and their own current skills and abilities) in order to be a better version of themselves tomorrow.

Dreaming and envisioning a new and brighter future has an amazingly attractive power that works as a catalyst and mobilizes these individuals to passionately and courageously act in the direction of their dreams.

One of the roles and responsibilities of a coach is to elicit, cajole, tempt, and even pull these visions and dreams out of their clients with powerful and provocative questions.

Exercise:

Create a list of engaging and powerful questions for yourself and those around you that will strengthen and grow your "dreaming muscle" to expand your potential to grow into your very best self.

#322: "Everyone thinks of changing the world but no one thinks of changing himself."

– Leo Tolstoy, Russian author

I have to admit it: I never took the time to read *War and Peace*, or *Anna Karenina*, two of Tolstoy's greatest novels. Maybe if Tolstoy was a blogger, I would be more versed in his work!

An interesting fact about him is that he was known as a moral thinker and social reformer. Some of his works are noted to have significantly impacted individuals such as Mahatma Gandhi and Martin Luther King, Jr.

Exercise:

What small or large changes can you make in yourself that will not only change your world but perhaps also the world around you?

#323: "The best use of life is love. The best expression of love is time. And the best time to love is now."

– Rick Warren, Christian pastor and author

www.rickwarren.org

In the world of business and executive coaching, the subject of love is rarely discussed in great depth. In the field of life or personal coaching, it's far more acceptable and often very welcomed.

Many coaches, including myself, believe that all coaching *is* life coaching, with variable degrees of focus on the areas of greatest importance. When you dig into these areas, of course, what you then discover is that foundation of love.

Exercise:

How can you stand on a foundation of love and give your time to those things you care deeply about – now?

#324: "It's not about an opening weekend. It's about a career, building a set of films you're proud of."

– George Clooney, American actor

If you were to win an award for lifetime achievement, what would the highlight reel contain before they introduced you?

In today's society, we seem enthralled with "one hit wonders" in many areas of life. We watch the hottest YouTube clips or we listen to the catchiest songs of the day. We focus on subjects that grab the headlines on the nightly news.

Clooney is suggesting we consider our enduring legacy as the effort and accomplishment over time that demonstrates staying power and some permanence.

Exercise:

What else do you want or need to accomplish in the year ahead to be worthy of your own lifetime achievement award?

#325: "Do what you love and love what you do. There's no better way to a happier you!"

– Dr. Seuss, American children's author

About a month ago, my wife Wendy gave me the gift of a "thought for the day" Dr. Seuss desk display. I have to admit that it wasn't until I was stumped for a good quote that I sought the wisdom of the dear doctor.

To me, the quote above is one of the most meaningful, as it points to the very nature of how we spend our time, and the level of happiness we experience through our vocations.

Exercise:

Download the Yes Magazine Happiness Poster entitled, *10 Things Science Says Will Make You Happy* from:

www.yesmagazine.org/pdf/48/Happiness_Poster11x17.pdf

... or email me at barry@dempcoaching.com and I will send it to you.

#326: "Live your truth. Express your love. Share your enthusiasm. Take action toward your dreams. Walk your talk. Dance and sing to your music. Embrace your blessings. Make today worth remembering."

– Steve Maraboli, American behavioral scientist and author

www.stevemaraboli.com

This quote packs quite a punch. It is actually eight bite-sized pieces of coaching stuck together. Take a moment to separate each of these nuggets of wisdom and see how well you are doing in each area by rating yourself on a 1–10 scale.

Exercise:

Select at least one of these areas you wish to enhance today and in the coming weeks, and identify a specific action or two that will take you to the next level.

Feel free to choose a second, third, etc.

#327: "Don't think *of* your goals – think *from* your goals."

– Unknown

Regardless of how much or even how little you've achieved over the past year or two, consider a new approach to setting goals for the future. This quote suggests that we use our goals as a magnet to attract and pull us forward in thoughts and deeds to realize them.

Exercise:

Begin with the end in mind and think from your goals and you will see the action steps and milestones more clearly than ever before.

Consider picking up a copy of Stephen Covey's famous book, *The 7 Habits of Highly Effective People,* and pay particular attention to Habit #2, which is, "Begin with the end [goals] in mind."

You may also wish to watch this video, which starts with the above quote: vimeo.com/23265082

#328: "Our brains become magnetized with the dominant thoughts we hold in our minds and by means with which no man is familiar, these 'magnets' attract to us the forces, the people and the circumstances of life which harmonize with the nature of our dominant thoughts."

– Napoleon Hill, American self-help author

I've broken one of my own guidelines to share this quote by Napoleon Hill. It is much longer than the quotes I normally use – and yet a fundamental premise of coaching is being willing to go outside your comfort zone, or break a pattern so a new world can emerge.

Perhaps by breaking a self-imposed rule here, I've simply embraced my own coaching in order to bring wise thinking to you and others.

Exercise:

There is a TV series on the science channel called Futurescape, narrated by James Woods. In one of the first episodes they reviewed research from New York University on the ability to read our thoughts.

What are your dominant thoughts and how are they manifesting in the reality of your life? If you could simply make a switch to a more entertaining, engaging, and prosperous "channel" in your life, what would the programming be?

#329: "Think before you speak. Words can get you into trouble much easier than they can get you out of it."

– D. Ernest Green (*attrib.*)

As part of my Personal Excellence Training, I spend a considerable amount of time developing each client's awareness of their inner voice. Sometimes this voice shows up as a judge or a critic when it is directed toward others or as a gremlin when it is directed inward.

The problem comes when this inner voice is not monitored for potential damage and is put on external speaker.

Exercise:

Today and over the next week, take particular note of when your inner voice is judgmental or critical. Ask yourself, "If I put these thoughts out there, will it forward the situation or simply make me feel justified and right?"

When your inner gremlin's voice is directed toward yourself, the damage is done without uttering a word. In this case, you need to catch the critical words in the formulation stage and reframe them to do no harm – or perhaps even to empower yourself in a positive direction.

#330: "As your consciousness expands, your level of expectation will grow. Keep asking yourself, 'Am I selling myself short?' Most of us are."

– John R. Spannuth, American swimmer

The coaching process usually helps people delve into new areas of perception, reconsidering their views of reality and what is possible. This expanded consciousness can either increase our courage to pursue new possibilities or generate fear which can make us stop – or even run in the opposite direction.

Exercise:

In what areas of your life are you selling yourself short due to fear?

How can you summon the courage of your expanded consciousness to foster and realize new possibilities in your professional and personal life?

#331: "We seldom think of what we have but always of what we lack."

– Arthur Schopenhauer, German philosopher

What do you think are the relative percentages of our focus on what we lack versus what we have? Are they 90/10, 80/20, 70/30, 60/40 or 50/50? You may notice I stopped at 50/50 – and for the purpose of this quote, let's just say that the odds, in general, aren't in most people's favor.

What is your own ratio?

Regardless of your own score, focusing your attention on what you already have is the key to happiness and living a fulfilling life.

Exercise:

For the next week, use a journal or notebook to record your thoughts on what you have and what you lack. Consider using an alarm (perhaps on your phone) to trigger you to capture these thoughts.

After writing about what you have, ask yourself, "What else?" and add even more to the list, to shift yourself toward a greater appreciation of the richness and abundance all around you.

#332: "If you ask me what I came to do in this world, I, an artist, will answer you: 'I am here to live out loud.'"

– Émile Zola, French naturalist writer

Consider for a moment that the journey of life is actually a form of art. Our lives contain many components, including work, family, community, and so on. Ask yourself, "How expressed and fulfilled do I feel in these (and other) domains?"

Many of us, including myself from time to time, live quiet, reserved lives which seem to provide some degree of protection, security, and safety. These perceived benefits have a considerable cost, in that they limit the upsides of life, including joy, love, excitement, adventure, and much more.

As a coach, husband, father, son, and community leader, I have decided to dare a bit more greatly and live a louder life.

Exercise:

Please let me know, by emailing barry@dempcoaching.com, how you will take on the challenge to pursue your own form of art and crank up the speakers to your life.

#333: "No man becomes rich unless he enriches others."

– Andrew Carnegie, Scottish-American industrialist

Andrew Carnegie led the enormous expansion of the American steel industry in the late 19th century.

He was also one of the most highly profiled philanthropists of his time. In an article he wrote, "The Gospel of Wealth", he called on other people of means to use their wealth to improve society.

Exercise:

Explore how you could contribute your own riches and resources, including gifts, talents, skills, and abilities to improve the lives of others.

As you give of yourself, you'll discover what Carnegie knew: your own life will become even richer.

#334: "I never hit a shot – not even in practice – without having a very sharp, in-focus picture of it in my head."

– Jack Nicklaus, American golfer

www.nicklaus.com

Jack Nicklaus is considered by many the best golfer of all time. His accomplishments are far too many to describe here. His quote above is great coaching for all of us looking to achieve mastery and excellence in any area we wish.

The power of a clear and compelling vision for some future event, even if it is a golf shot, is fundamental to mobilizing our thoughts and actions to make it so. Nicklaus and most people of great achievement seem to have a razor-sharp consistent and persistent ability to concentrate and focus on the prize.

Exercise:

Revisit the pivot point/self-coaching exercise first described in Quote #193.

Use it to clearly determine your current reality, envision a sharp and focused future, and then, like Nicklaus, take the shot toward your goal.

Don't be surprised if you hit your mark more often than ever before.

#335: "The greatest mistake you can make in life is to continually be afraid you will make one."

– Elbert Hubbard, American writer, artist and philosopher

In the assessment process I undertake prior to each coaching agreement, I pay particular attention to the challenges and obstacles that may be limiting my client's success.

We do identify many external factors that aren't always in their control, yet it is surprising to discover the numerous internal barriers that limit their success and overall life satisfaction. Among these internal obstacles is the often crippling fear of making a mistake and failing – which often prevents them from ever trying something new in the first place.

Exercise:

Where specifically are you currently stopped by the fear of making a mistake or failing? Find a coach, friend, family member, or mentor to help you summon the courage to work through these fears.

Sometimes, it is helpful to use the acronym "**FEAR**" which stands for "**F**alse **E**vidence **A**ppearing **R**eal."

#336: "Life lived for tomorrow will always be just a day away from being realized."

– Leo Buscaglia, aka "Dr. Love", American author and motivational speaker

Anticipation, expectation, and the promise of a better tomorrow are powerful forces that can mobilize us to call forth our most committed efforts.

On the other hand, consider happiness, joy, fulfillment, and satisfaction. These emotions are primarily experienced in the moment and not in the future.

Far too many people lose sight of what is just in front of their noses because they are gazing off over the horizons of life.

Exercise:

Regardless of whether you are near-sighted, far-sighted, or have perfect vision, how will you take the time to look all around today, to experience the fullest expression of each and every moment?

#337: "Live neither in the past nor in the future, but let each day's work absorb all your interest, energy and enthusiasm."

– William Osler, Canadian physician

In his book, *Drive*, Daniel Pink describes three predominant qualities to life that drive all of us. They include:

1. **Autonomy** – the ability to influence our world

2. **Mastery** – the capacity to grow and improve our skills and abilities

3. **Purpose** – a sense of meaning – knowing that our daily efforts are making a difference to our own lives and the lives of others

Exercise:

Using the three qualities above as a framework for a driven life, how do you plan to focus your interest, energy, and enthusiasm today?

#338: "Holding on to anger is like grasping a hot coal with the intent of throwing it at someone else. You are the only one who gets burned."

– Buddhaghosa, Indian commentator on Buddha's work

No one in their right mind would ever pick up a hot coal to throw it at someone. In an instant, they would be raced off to the emergency room for treatment, and a very protracted recovery period. Most likely they would also bear considerable scars that would remain for years or perhaps for life.

Exercise:

Take note of the times when you observe the destructive force of anger today.

How can you minimize it, release it, or better yet, replace it with understanding, tolerance, and forgiveness – to make for a more peaceful, accepting, and loving world?

#339: "Happiness, that grand mistress of the ceremonies in the dance of life, impels us through all its mazes and meanderings, but leads none of us by the same route."

– Charles Caleb Colton, English cleric, writer and collector

Recently, I began watching a TV series on the National Geographic channel, "Life Below Zero." The storyline follows the life of four different families living in Northern Alaska in one of the harshest and coldest environments possible.

What makes this show so interesting and intriguing for me is how passionate they all are about their lifestyle, and how happy they all are with their choices, despite the considerable hardship of living off the land in the rugged Alaskan wilderness.

Exercise:

What is your current route toward happiness? How can you better embrace the mazes and meanderings that are leading you on your own unique journey?

#340: "After climbing a great hill, one only finds that there are many more hills to climb."

– Nelson Mandela, South African anti-apartheid President

At the end of 2013, the world celebrated the long and remarkable life and legacy of Nelson Mandela.

If he were a mountain climber, he would perhaps have scaled more summits than almost anyone in history, and he taught us the important life lesson that it's all about climbing.

Exercise:

What hills and mountains have you already climbed, where you have stood at the summit with a feeling of satisfaction and accomplishment?

What new hills are before you to challenge your strength and resolve, to further your life journey and your contribution to the world?

#341: "For fast acting relief, try slowing down."

– Lily Tomlin, American actress and comedian

www.lilytomlin.com

When I was young, I remember a corny television commercial for Alka-Seltzer. The little jingle that promoted it was, "Plop, plop, fizz, fizz, oh what a relief it is!" Catchy, huh?

Whenever you wish a bit of relief from the onslaught of life, Tomlin suggests that slowing down may be just the medicine to do the trick.

Exercise:

In what areas of your life do you need to take your foot off the gas and apply the break to experience the relief that you desire?

Who are the coaches, mentors, friends, and family members that can help you throttle back?

#342: "The man is a success who has lived well, laughed often, and loved much."

– Robert Louis Stevenson, Scottish writer

As I write this, it is a Saturday morning following the Christmas and New Year holiday and I am reflecting fondly on the memory of the time I've just spent with those closest to me. I am feeling a wonderful sense of success because we all lived well, laughed often, and loved much during this time.

Exercise:

My challenge to you (and myself as well) is to plan to live more successfully based on Stevenson's criteria – throughout the year, not just during those infrequent special holiday times and gatherings.

#343: "No one would ever have crossed the ocean if he could have gotten off the ship in the storm."

– Charles Kettering, American inventor and businessman

Virtually no one I've ever met has had a life of smooth sailing. Just think about the storms that you've faced over the years. If you are reading this book, you must have weathered things reasonably well.

Consider life's challenges as tests to you, as a sailor of life's seas, to cross your own personal and professional oceans. If you get off the ship too early, you have literally missed the ride of your life!

Exercise:

Select at least one personal and one professional ocean you intend to navigate in the year ahead. What preparations can you make for stormy weather?

#344: "Look at everything as though you are seeing it for the first time, with the eyes of a child, fresh with wonder."

– Joseph Cornell, American artist and sculptor

It's January 4th and I've just returned from my morning workout at my local fitness center. Guess what I found? You're right – lots of new faces intending to start off the new year with a renewed commitment to their fitness and well being.

The annual New Year celebration in Times Square often includes an aging Father Time and a newborn representing the year ahead.

Take Cornell's coaching here and begin by looking at all things in the light of wonder and possibility, to make the coming months or years your best ever.

Exercise:

Look at your current vocation, avocations, relationships, habits, and even your food choices, and explore tasting and experiencing all of these with a fresh new perspective.

#345: "Growth and comfort seldom ride the same horse."

– Unknown

When I was a small boy, I went to a carnival where I had the opportunity to ride a pony. (For the sake of this quote, let's call the pony a small horse.) The initial aspect of walking in a circle at a slow pace was enjoyable – however, I found that my bottom got a bit of a jolt when we worked our way up to a trot!

At the start of a new year, very few of us wish to kick things off at a walking pace. Our goals are far more ambitious – and we must gallop forward to reach them with urgency.

This quote suggests that we be prepared for a rough and sometimes bumpy ride to reach our destination before the setting sun.

Exercise:

Identify between two and three primary goals you have for the coming year where you are fully prepared for the possibility of a rough ride.

Share these goals with a coach, mentor, colleague, or family member who will support your efforts to reach your destination.

#346: "Teaching is an instinctual art, mindful of potential, craving of realization, a pausing, seamless process."

– A. Bartlett Giamatti, American educator

We have all heard the quote, "When the student is ready, the teacher will appear."

Think for a moment about the times when this quote has been most apparent in your own life. How often were you the student? How often were you the teacher?

Exercise:

Consider how we are always experiencing being both the student and the teacher in a seamless tapestry of continuous learning.

In the year ahead, how will you be the student and the teacher in your life and in the lives of others, to fully pursue the boundless possibilities and potential in yourself and in those around you?

#347: "Try brushing your teeth tonight with your other hand."

– Ken Burns, American documentary filmmaker

Wendy and I recently spent the holidays in Madison, Wisconsin with both of our children and their new spouses. Navigating the roads in this area was a new experience, even with GPS. My sense of direction was off for most of the visit.

It is estimated that about 90% of all of our behaviors are based on our habits and even the small act of brushing our teeth with the opposite hand can feel quite awkward.

The opportunity to see new sights and have many varied and different experiences during our vacation was definitely worth this awkward feeling.

Exercise:

What are some of the small and perhaps large changes you plan to make that will have you see wonderful new sights and experience memorable opportunities ahead?

#348: "The greatest story you will ever tell is your own."

– Charlie Rose, American broadcast journalist

A few years ago, our family started a new tradition of taking one day over the holidays as a "movie marathon day" where we all see the top movies back-to-back from early morning until midnight.

In 2013, it was five in a row, but in previous years some of the gang saw as many as six or seven. We all love to be carried away by the drama, romance, and humor of these wonderful stories.

Exercise:

During this month, please take about 15–30 minutes to do a "year in review" to identify the signature stories that would make up your highlight reel of the past year.

Take another 15–30 minutes to script out your coming attractions for the year ahead, doing your best to make sure it would be nominated for your best year ever.

#349: "Kindred spirits are not so scarce as I used to think. It's splendid to find out there are so many of them in the world."

– L.M. Montgomery, Canadian author

How do you find a kindred spirit? It might appear difficult if you believe that things of the spirit world are invisible.

Consider the scientific corollary of the electromagnetic spectrum of light. Even the visible spectrum of light is invisible without a prism to show us the beautiful colors within. Perhaps we as human-beings each have a "rainbow-making" capacity to help us reveal these kindred spirits.

Exercise:

Imagine you are a radio transmitter that can deliver into the world your invisible signal powered by your vision, value, beliefs, and passions. People who can pick up these signals without static and from considerable distances are your kindred spirits.

It just happens that you are also a radio receiver with the power to tune in and receive the signals sent by others.

Montgomery is suggesting here that if we are very intentional about our transmitting and receiving, we will be surprised by just how kindred the human spirit really is.

#350: "You stand at a boundary [...] You stand between whatever binds you to your past and whatever might be unbounded in your future."

– Seamus Heaney, Irish poet and playwright

Taking stock of the past can be a useful exercise to discover lessons learned, mistakes not to repeat, and places where you have succeeded, where you have considerable momentum to carry you forward.

Exploring the possibilities of an unbounded future in the various domains of your life can be very energizing and exciting. Tap into your courage, boldness, passion, and values to make this future come true.

Exercise:

Select a coach, mentor, friend, family member, or colleague to talk to about the unbounded possibilities of your future. Buy them a cup of coffee – or better yet, take them out for a meal. This is not an exercise you want to rush.

For extra credit, consider meeting with this person at least once a month to explore your efforts and progress throughout the year.

#351: "No plan is worth the paper it is printed on unless it starts you doing something."

– William Danforth, co-founder of the American Youth Federation

January is one of the busiest times for coaches, when both individuals and organizations crystallize and clarify their goals and plans for the new year. Of course, we have all seen these intentions and plans lose their steam and sit on the shelf to eventually await the next planning cycle, when we do it all over again.

When asked, a very significant percentage of professionals would describe the planning process as "unremarkable" and "not particularly worthwhile" – primarily due to the lack of ongoing review and rigorous execution.

Exercise:

Seek out the help of your own individual or organizational coaches to make sure that this year, your plans are worth their weight in gold.

If you do not yet have a coach, consider taking a look at the services I offer at www.dempcoaching.com/professional-services.

#352: "It was only a sunny smile and little it cost in the giving, but like morning light, it scattered the night and made the day worth living."

– F. Scott Fitzgerald, American author

Winter here in Michigan began about a month ago, and along with some of the coldest temperatures in the area due to the Arctic vortex effect, we are experiencing days with the least amount of daylight of the entire year.

A reasonable number of people are affected to some degree in their mood and outlook by the lack of daylight. Some experience a syndrome, Seasonal Affective Disorder, that can cause low energy, moodiness, and even depression. You can find out more about this here:

en.wikipedia.org/wiki/Seasonal_affective_disorder

Exercise:

Each time you offer or receive a low-cost smile today, think of it as a form of light therapy to help you and others "spring forward" – just as if you were beginning your own personal daylight saving time.

#353: "Passion is energy. Feel the power that comes from focusing on what excites you."

– Oprah Winfrey, talk show host and actress

Oprah Winfrey sets a wonderful example of a person of passion. From her early years in broadcasting to her 25 amazing years with her own network show, she lived and worked true to these words.

How passionate are you? What is it like for you on Sunday evening or on Monday morning as you embark on the day ahead?

Exercise:

Pay particular attention to your daily levels of passion, energy, and excitement. They are barometers for a fully engaged life.

Be prepared to make some needed changes and to become your own "weather forecaster", paying attention to these barometers so you can have that feeling of living a powerful and passionate life.

#354: "There is nothing that makes its way more directly to the soul than beauty."

– Joseph Addison, English writer and politician

Beauty has a way of stopping me in my tracks. The past few days here in Michigan have been filled with snow. The beautiful white blanket has literally stopped me from my usual routine of working out at the health club and doing a variety of errands.

Slowing down and taking a few extra moments to embrace this beautiful sight seems to connect me with a deeper experience of being in the world, which I find very important. Unfortunately, many of us, including myself, have to be forced to stop in order to take note of this beauty and the accompanying soulful experience.

Exercise:

Imagine that you are a "beauty detector", similar to a metal detector. When you come across some beauty, stop and "dig it up" to experience more of the treasures available.

#355: "The pleasure of doing a thing in the same way at the same time every day and savoring it should be noted."

– Arnold Bennett, English writer

Coaching often has a lot to do with breaking patterns so that new worlds will emerge. See my blog for more on this:

www.thequotablecoach.com/coaching-2/patterns-change-time-audio

Bennett's quote has an appeal in that doing the same thing over and over again the same way at the same time each day can have considerable merits. A daily rhythm of behaviors to provide consistency, stability, and a general foundation for the rest of our diverse and wildly varied lives can be compared to a strong building's foundation or a tree's root system and trunk.

Exercise:

What current daily habits and behaviors do you currently have that simply work well for you?

What new or additional daily rituals can you embrace or engage in that will make you feel even more centered and happy?

#356: "Your greatness is measured by your horizons."

– Michelangelo, Renaissance sculptor and painter

When was the last time you watched the weather report on the evening news? In addition to temperature, humidity, wind speed, and chance of precipitation, they sometimes include "visibility", which is the distance one can see clearly toward the horizon.

I'd like you to consider not only how far you can see into the distance, but also what you view when doing so. The inspirational and vivid goals within your horizons, as Michelangelo suggests, can be the fuel of greatness.

Exercise:

Imagine that you have the capacity to expand your vision's clarity and distance, viewing your personal horizons through a telescopic or binocular device.

What horizons do you see that will be the measure of your greatness in the days and weeks ahead?

#357: "Great people are not affected by each puff of wind that blows ill. Like great ships, they sail serenely on, in a calm sea or a great tempest."

– George Washington, first President of the United States

Have you ever attended a cruise ship orientation? In addition to learning all the fascinating statistics about these floating cities, you will almost always find out about their technology – which includes a very sophisticated set of navigation and stability control capabilities.

It's remarkable that the crew can get these great ships from point A to point B with minimal disturbance to the passengers' enjoyment.

How often are you negatively affected by those small (and not so small) puffs of wind in your daily activities? How often do you experience bouts of seasickness that upset your day?

Exercise:

What factors in your world help create your own personal stability control center that can help you sail through life in a more serene and calm manner?

#358: "It's not what you say, it's what they hear that counts."

– Unknown

Learning how to communicate effectively is perhaps the highest priority for most individuals and organizations entering a coaching relationship. This may not be what they originally emphasize in the first meeting – instead they tell the coach they want to improve sales, productivity, and quality.

However, beneath most forms of achievement is a foundation of effective communication – and a critical subset of it is to truly hear and understand others. A technique to improve your odds of being heard is to practice and master the art of listening to others first.

Listening to others is like emptying the other person's "expression cup." When we let others fully express their ideas, we create space for our opinions to enter the open spaces in their minds – especially if these are on the same topic as their ideas.

Exercise:

To turbo-charge your relationship skills and your communication mastery in the year ahead, look to your own ability to honor each and everyone you meet. Seek to listen and understand others before you seek to be heard by them.

You may wish to download my Masterful Relationships workbook, which includes some extra guidance on active listening. Go to www.dempcoaching.com/download-your-free-workbooks and enter the password **barrydemp** (all lower-case).

#359: "Rain and sun are to the flower as praise and encouragement are to the human spirit."

– Unknown

As a former science teacher, I am fascinated by the process of photosynthesis – that plants can use sunlight to make their own food seems nothing short of a miracle.

Man (and virtually all animals) eat these plants as our own way of feeding ourselves and sustaining life. Yet we are feeding only the body portion of ourselves – leaving our souls and spirits a bit empty.

Exercise:

How can you feed others the important nutrient of praise and acknowledgement, and surround yourself with others who will offer it to you in return?

#360: "Finish each day and be done with it. You have done what you could. Some blunders and absurdities have crept in; forget them as soon as you can. Tomorrow is a new day. You shall begin it serenely and with too high a spirit to be encumbered with your old nonsense."

– Ralph Waldo Emerson, writer and philosopher

I have a pet peeve: receiving the answer, "Not bad", when I ask someone how they're doing. What constitutes a "bad" day and what exactly does "not bad" actually mean? Sure, we all have those days when things don't go exactly as we planned – in fact, they rarely do. The question to ponder here is how upset you get when this occurs.

Consider daily blunders and absurdities as very tiny leaks from a great glass of your favorite beverage. No matter what happens, you can always maintain at least a half-full perspective, knowing that each new day starts overflowing with possibilities.

Exercise:

Try on the idea of, "What you get done each day is what you get done," and learn to be satisfied with whatever shows up. With each new day, consciously choose to be fully alive.

#361: "A balanced diet is a chocolate in each hand."

– Unknown

Chocolate is considered a superfood with about five out of seven people worldwide enjoying it very much. I am one of them! (Some people believe it should even be its own food group...)

Below are some interesting facts to consider when enjoying this treat:

- It can decrease the risk of stroke.
- It can boost heart health.
- It can fill you up and keep you full so you don't overeat.
- It may reduce the risk of diabetes.
- It may offer protection from UV rays and skin damage.
- It can quiet a cough.
- It can boost your mood – it does mine.
- It can improve blood flow.
- It can enhance your vision.
- It can even boost your brainpower and make you smarter.

Exercise:

If you enjoy it too, look for ways to moderately include chocolate in your life to make it a bit sweeter. To learn more, check out the Huffington Post article, "10 Health Benefits of Chocolate."

#362: "With brains, heart, and courage, you can achieve anything you desire."

– Inspired by *The Wizard of Oz*

When I was a young boy, my family loved *The Wizard of Oz*. This movie, with its black and white to vivid color transition, amazed all of us with both the images and the compelling story.

If it's one of your favorites too, you will recall Dorothy's journey along with the Scarecrow, Tin Man, and Cowardly Lion to reach the great and powerful Wizard of Oz.

Of course, the storyline also involves the Scarecrow discovering his brain, the Tin Man finding his heart, and the Lion embracing his courage.

Exercise:

What habits and practices can you develop and undertake in order to fully use your brain, heart, and courage to fully achieve your greatest desires?

#363: "There are people whose clocks stop at a certain point in their lives."

– Charles Augustin Sainte-Beuve, French literary critic

As I sit in my favorite chair writing this, it's Sunday, February 2nd. That's right, it's Groundhog Day.

I'm not going to refer to that little furry creature, Punxsutawney Phil, and whether he saw his shadow. Instead, I want to describe the movie, *Groundhog Day*, starring Bill Murray, which is a bit of a guilty pleasure.

If you've not seen the (ahem) "masterpiece", the moral of the story is that until Phil Connors (Bill Murray) changes his ways, he will be destined to live a life that is making him a bit insane by being the same person he's always been before – i.e. his clock has stopped.

Exercise:

How can you put a fresh battery in your life clock to make the very most of the time remaining to live life to its fullest?

#364: "The true university of these days is a collection of books."

– Thomas Carlyle, Scottish philosopher and writer

Thomas Carlyle was born in 1795. He was a Scottish philosopher, satirical writer, essayist, historian, and teacher during the Victorian era.

What do you think Carlyle's quote might say if he lived today in the era of Google, mobile apps, and voice recognition software? He would undoubtedly have included blogs, audio, video, and a host of other modalities from which to choose.

Exercise:

Consider watching the 1959 Twilight Zone episode, "Time Enough at Last", where the main character, the coke-bottle-glasses-wearing Henry Bemis, explores his voracious appetite to read and learn.

What are your preferred methods of educating yourself in this time of such variety?

How can you make a bit more time for your own pursuit of continuous learning and take a self-declared advanced degree in any subject you choose?

#365: "Quotable quotes are coins rubbed smooth by circulation."

– Louis Menand, writer and academic

One of the great things about coaching is that its impact is "sticky" and often produces a sustainable, long-lasting difference in the lives of those involved. However, many people find it difficult to receive an adequate level of coaching support in their vocational and personal lives.

Powerful and highly memorable quotes are one solution, and the more they circulate through the written and spoken word, the more life's edges are smoothed.

Exercise:

Use the index of this book to find the category of quotes that has the greatest value for you at this point in your life.

Capture a least a few of your favorites and share them with people who will be supportive of your efforts.

A Final Word

I hope you've enjoyed *The Quotable Coach: Daily Nuggets of Practical Wisdom*. If you would take the time to write a quick review on Goodreads or Amazon, I would be very grateful. Thanks in advance.

To get more quotes delivered on a daily basis (Monday – Friday), simply visit www.thequotablecoach.com and enter your name and email address on the right hand side.

If you'd like to go further with your professional and/or personal development, I would be delighted to work with you. Please visit my website at www.dempcoaching.com for information about working with me, or feel free to email me at barry@dempcoaching.com or call me at 248-740-3231.

Wishing you all the best on your journey through life,

Barry Demp

Acknowledgements

For as long as I can remember, my wife Wendy has been telling me that there's a book in me. Over the course of many years, she's encouraged me, believed in me, and provided her ongoing support and advocacy. She is my biggest fan, and this book would never have been written without her.

In addition, Wendy has been invaluable as a co-editor. Her commitment to accuracy had her work very long hours to correct typos, suggest improvements, check facts, and make *The Quotable Coach: Daily Nuggets of Practical Wisdom* the very best it can be. Wendy, thank you so much!

A special thanks goes out to my amazing writing coach, Ali Luke, whose support and writing talents have helped me offer you this work. Ali has also worked with me for over two years to bring The Quotable Coach series to your email inboxes on a daily basis. Ali, thanks for all your hard work and partnership!

Another special thank you also goes out to my social media, search engine optimization, and web design associate, Judd Seida. He has been a valuable sounding-board and advocate throughout this entire process.

A big thanks as well to my family, friends, clients, colleagues, and everyone who voted for their favorite title and cover artwork for this book.

Of course, this book would not have been possible without the contributions of over 300 people quoted within (some more than once). Many thanks to everyone included for their words of wisdom.

Copyright Notice

Index

Achievements

#316: "The race will go to..."

#324: "It's not about an opening..."

#340: "After climbing a great hill..."

#348: "The greatest story..."

Action

#2: "You're more likely to act yourself..."

#9: "Success in life comes not from..."

#11: "God, grant me the serenity..."

#17: "Do what you can, with what..."

#38: "Not everything that is faced..."

#43: "You cannot dream yourself..."

#46: "You cannot talk your way out..."

#48: "Nothing happens unless first..."

#59: "Shoot for the moon..."

#61: "Whatever you vividly imagine..."

#100: "Even if you're on the right track..."

#113: "Well done is better than well said."

#168: "If you chase two rabbits..."

#178: "Opportunities are like sunrises..."

#193: "It is common sense to take..."

#196: "The only things that stand..."

#213: "Follow effective action with..."

#219: "You will never stub your toe..."

#225: "Today is when everything..."

#242: "At the end of each day..."

#264: "Try something different..."

#290: "Action conquers fear."

#299: "The best thing about the future..."

#308: "Character is revealed by action..."

#319: "The gratification comes..."

#351: "No plan is worth the paper..."

Aging

#58: "Autumn is a second spring..."

#74: "Hardening of the heart..."

#81: "The bad news is time flies..."

#96: "Often the greatest enemy of..."

#153: "Though face and form alter with..."

#159: "Life is short. Do not forget about..."

#177: "Someday is not a day of the week."

#230: "How far you go in life depends..."

#234: "What becomes fragile when..."

#284: "An apple a day..."

#363: "There are people whose clocks..."

Attitude

#109: "Things turn out the best for the people..."

#216: "When we are no longer able..."

#297: "Constant kindness can..."

#309: "People often say that motivation..."

Beauty

#55: "The work will wait while you show..."

#58: "Autumn is a second spring..."

#92: "When love and skill work together..."

#153: "Though face and form alter with..."

#178: "Opportunities are like sunrises..."

#215: "There is, indeed, something..."

#245: "It's on the strength of observation..."

#288: "Instead of seeking new landscapes..."

#344: "Look at everything as though..."

#354: "There is nothing that makes..."

Belief

#196: "The only things that stand..."

#301: "Optimism is the faith that..."

Breakthroughs

#14: "If we were to do all we are capable..."

#21: "Nothing ventured, nothing gained."

#116: "A great pleasure in life is doing..."

#126: "A friend is a loved one who..."

#292: "If an egg is broken by outside force..."

#305: "Our business in life is not..."

#314: "What we see when watching..."

#318: "People will cling to an unsatisfactory..."

Challenges

#10: "Every problem introduces..."

#16: "The tests of life..."

#25: "When the student is ready..."

#30: "Good timber does not..."

#121: "Adversity reveals genius..."

#128: "Our greatest glory consists not in..."

Change

Character

#150: "When a man is wrapped up..."

#182: "The highest reward for a person's toil..."

#214: "I get a chance to be anyone..."

#243: "Try to be like the turtle..."

#308: "Character is revealed by action..."

#313: "There's only one corner of..."

#317: "Habit is the daily battle-ground of character."

#322: "Everyone thinks of changing..."

#357: "Great people are not affected..."

Children

#55: "The work will wait while you show..."

#71: "Just do what you do best."

#149: "Don't worry that children never..."

#172: "Cherish your visions and..."

#224: "One's first step in wisdom is to..."

#237: "If you judge a fish by its ability to…"

Choices

#4: "It's not what you've got..."

#12: "Concentrate all your thoughts..."

#158: "Life is all about choices..."

#198: "It's choice – not chance – that determines..."

#269: "Only dead fish swim with..."

#278: "Every human has four endowments..."

Coaching

#7: "The wise man questions himself..."

#15: "The greatest good you..."

#16: "The tests of life..."

#32: "You can't help someone..."

#71: "Just do what you do best."

#85: "In everyone's life, at some time..."

#105: "The only limit to our realization..."

#115: "Our chief want in life is somebody..."

#130: "Act so as to elicit the best in others..."

#133: "There are some people who live..."

#136: "I know of no more encouraging fact..."

#144: "You have to have your heart in..."

#152: "Tell me and I'll forget..."

#162: "Most people live..."

#176: "The older I get the less I listen..."

#184: "Hard work without talent is a shame..."

#200: "If we only listened with..."

#228: "A 'coach' remains something or someone who..."

#235: "You may have a fresh start..."

#251: "The key is to keep company only..."

#258: "Always bear in mind that your own..."

#271: "A prudent question is one-half of wisdom."

#277: "An investment in knowledge..."

#292: "If an egg is broken by outside force..."

#301: "Optimism is the faith that..."

#304: "Lighthouses don't go running..."

#310: "I keep six honest serving-men..."

#315: "A good head and a good heart..."

#321: "Dreams are powerful..."

#326: "Live your truth. Express your love..."

#351: "No plan is worth the paper..."

#365: "Quotable quotes are..."

Commitment

#27: "A man should conceive of..."

#112: "To dream anything that you want..."

#117: "The quality of a person's life is..."

#156: "Far away there in the sunshine..."

Conformity

#65: "Life is a great big canvas..."

#294: "I believe in getting into..."

Courage

#22: "Our doubts are traitors..."

#105: "The only limit to our realization..."

#157: "Keep knocking and the joy inside..."

#160: "If there is something to gain..."

#163: "Remember that failure is an event..."

#165: "The Universe favors the brave..."

#194: "Courage does not always roar..."

#202: "Do not follow where the path..."

#219: "You will never stub your toe..."

#233: "One can choose to go back..."

#246: "The first to apologize is..."

#282: "There can be no joy..."

#330: "As your consciousness expands..."

#362: "With brains, heart, and courage..."

Creativity

#42: "Change the way you look..."

#60: "To raise new questions..."

#65: "Life is a great big canvas..."

#69: "Ah, but a man's reach should..."

#79: "Creativity involves breaking out..."

#93: "Rules and models destroy..."

#272: "One thought driven home..."

#283: "Words are small shapes in..."

#288: "Instead of seeking new landscapes..."

#312: "All words are pegs..."

#332: "If you ask me what I came..."

Decisions

#51: "When at a conflict between..."

#181: "People don't buy for logical reasons..."

Effort

#18: "I firmly believe that any..."

#66: "Is the juice worth the squeezing?"

#95: "There is a giant asleep within everyone..."

#98: "There are no shortcuts to..."

#102: "The difference between ordinary..."

#238: "It is better to be prepared for..."

#242: "At the end of each day..."

#276: "If a man does his best..."

#299: "The best thing about the future..."

#313: "There's only one corner of..."

#315: "A good head and a good heart..."

#319: "The gratification comes..."

Encouragement

#28: "As human beings, our job..."

#41: "How far that little candle..."

#167: "I have yet to find the man..."

#359: "Rain and sun are to the flower..."

Excellence

#8: "The hallmark of excellence..."

#14: "If we were to do all we are capable..."

#72: "A man's life is interesting primarily..."

#117: "The quality of a person's life is..."

#139: "When you are tough on yourself..."

#161: "Life is no brief candle for me..."

#169: "A successful man is one who..."

#209: "We are what we repeatedly..."

Experience

#19: "Experience is a hard..."

#227: "To know the road ahead..."

Failure

#47: "Remember to pick something up..."

#72: "A man's life is interesting primarily..."

#97: "Mishaps are like knives, that either..."

#119: "Far better it is to dare mighty things..."

#125: "Life is no straight and easy corridor..."

#128: "Our greatest glory consists not in..."

#146: "I don't measure a man's success..."

#147: "Do not look where you fell..."

#163: "Remember that failure is an event..."

#193: "It is common sense to take..."

#235: "You may have a fresh start..."

Fear

#22: "Our doubts are traitors..."

#52: "Progress is impossible without..."

#129: "Become so wrapped up in something..."

#236: "I have lived a long life and..."

#290: "Action conquers fear."

#335: "The greatest mistake you can make..."

Focus

#5: "Don't stumble over something..."

#12: "Concentrate all your thoughts..."

#68: "If you do everything calmly..."

#168: "If you chase two rabbits..."

#190: "Nothing contributes so much..."

#283: "Words are small shapes in..."

#291: "It is not a daily increase..."

#328: "Our brains become magnetized..."

#331: "We seldom think of what..."

#334: "I never hit a shot..."

#336: "Life lived for tomorrow..."

Friendship

#57: "If you go looking for a friend..."

#67: "Friendship is a soul dwelling..."

#88: "Friendships multiply joys..."

#126: "A friend is a loved one who..."

#298: "A true friend never gets..."

Future

#17: "Do what you can, with what..."

#44: "Learn from yesterday..."

#48: "Nothing happens unless first..."

#69: "Ah, but a man's reach should..."

#71: "Just do what you do best."

#75: "Don't judge each day by..."

#82: "The ultimate test of a man's conscience..."

#123: "There is no medicine like hope..."

#141: "The employer generally gets..."

#161: "Life is no brief candle for me..."

#170: "It is only possible to live happily..."

#177: "Someday is not a day of the week."

#187: "Cease to inquire what the future..."

#205: "Time is the coin of..."

#225: "Today is when everything..."

#271: "A prudent question is one-half of wisdom."

#299: "The best thing about the future..."

#303: "We forfeit three-quarters..."

#305: "Our business in life is not..."

#337: "Live neither in the past nor..."

#350: "You stand at a boundary..."

Generosity

#32: "You can't help someone..."

#151: "No person was ever honored..."

#155: "In about the same degree as you..."

#220: "It is by spending oneself..."

#231: "The heart that gives, gathers."

#257: "You can rest assured that if you..."

#268: "When you're presented with the opportunity…"

#333: "No man becomes rich..."

Goals

#33: "In the confrontation between..."

#59: "Shoot for the moon..."

#137: "You read a book from beginning..."

#156: "Far away there in the sunshine..."

#198: "It's choice – not chance – that determines..."

#229: "I have one life and one chance..."

#252: "Dream big, but allow yourself..."

#261: "Discipline is the bridge between..."

#327: "Don't think *of* your goals..."

#345: "Growth and comfort..."

#351: "No plan is worth the paper..."

#356: "Your greatness is..."

Gratitude

#31: "Happiness cannot be traveled to..."

#64: "Be thankful for what you have..."

#74: "Hardening of the heart..."

#154: "Yesterday is history..."

#187: "Cease to inquire what the future..."

#201: "The best things in life..."

#281: "When it comes to life..."

#331: "We seldom think of what..."

Growth

#3: "People are anxious to improve..."

#30: "Good timber does not..."

#37: "There is nothing noble in..."

#54: "The longest journey is the..."

#63: "There are powers inside of you..."

#73: "Be always at war with your vices..."

#78: "To finish the moment..."

#89: "Death is Nature's expert advice..."

#95: "There is a giant asleep within everyone..."

#101: "One's mind, once stretched by a new idea..."

#111: "Quality is never an accident..."

#112: "To dream anything that you want..."

#118: "People seldom improve when they..."

#162: "Most people live..."

#165: "The Universe favors the brave..."

#179: "Good, better, best. Never let it rest..."

#189: "The universe will fill your cup..."

#214: "I get a chance to be anyone..."

#218: "If you won't be better tomorrow..."

#233: "One can choose to go back..."

#241: "If you can tell me who..."

#254: "We are betrayed by what is false within."

#267: "How am I doing?"

#285: "Problems are in your life..."

#287: "The optimist already sees..."

#345: "Growth and comfort..."

Habits

#2: "You're more likely to act yourself..."

#40: "It's not what we eat but..."

#73: "Be always at war with your vices..."

#209: "We are what we repeatedly..."

#211: "A bad habit never goes away..."

#317: "Habit is the daily battle-ground of character."

#347: "Try brushing your teeth..."

#355: "The pleasure of doing a thing..."

#362: "With brains, heart, and courage..."

Happiness

#31: "Happiness cannot be traveled to..."

#86: "It has been my observation that people..."

#88: "Friendships multiply joys..."

#94: "Make happy those who are near..."

#96: "Often the greatest enemy of..."

#106: "Happiness is not a state to arrive at..."

#108: "Most great men and women are not..."

#155: "In about the same degree as you..."

#170: "It is only possible to live happily..."

#191: "Happiness is a state of consciousness..."

#197: "Enjoy the little things..."

#246: "The first to apologize is..."

#325: "Do what you love and..."

#336: "Life lived for tomorrow..."

#339: "Happiness, that grand mistress..."

#352: "It was only a sunny smile..."

#355: "The pleasure of doing a thing..."

#361: "A balanced diet is a chocolate..."

Health

#284: "An apple a day..."

#352: "It was only a sunny smile..."

#361: "A balanced diet is a chocolate..."

Humor

#49: "To succeed in life, you need..."

#195: "Laughter is an instant vacation."

#256: "Imagination is a quality given..."

#263: "I learned that when I made..."

#273: "A smile is a curve..."

#295: "A lesson taught with humor..."

#342: "The man is a success..."

Inspiration

#131: "In the face of uncertainty..."

#215: "There is, indeed, something..."

#241: "If you can tell me who..."

#247: "Genius is no more than..."

#348: "The greatest story..."

#354: "There is nothing that makes..."

Integrity

#40: "It's not what we eat but..."

#41: "How far that little candle..."

#110: "Character is like a tree and reputation..."

#149: "Don't worry that children never..."

#176: "The older I get the less I listen..."

#206: "I long to accomplish..."

#221: "An uneasy conscience is..."

#249: "The merit of originality..."

#275: "There's no greater power..."

#286: "The world has a habit..."

#307: "Don't compromise yourself..."

Journeying

Leadership

#39: "Go to the people..."

#130: "Act so as to elicit the best in others..."

#358: "It's not what you say..."

Learning

#19: "Experience is a hard..."

#25: "When the student is ready..."

#36: "If I am walking with two..."

#44: "Learn from yesterday..."

#47: "Remember to pick something up..."

#97: "Mishaps are like knives, that either..."

#114: "It's what you learn after you..."

#147: "Do not look where you fell..."

#152: "Tell me and I'll forget..."

#185: "Reading one book is like..."

#208: "A man only learns in..."

#240: "A single conversation with a wise man..."

#277: "An investment in knowledge..."

#289: "We should learn from..."

#295: "A lesson taught with humor..."

#320: "If you can't explain it to..."

#346: "Teaching is an instinctual art..."

#364: "The true university of these days..."

Legacy

#206: "I long to accomplish..."

#229: "I have one life and one chance..."

#244: "The great secret of success..."

#324: "It's not about an opening..."

#340: "After climbing a great hill..."

Listening

#87: "The way of a fool is right..."

#166: "Be more concerned about..."

#188: "You'll never really understand..."

#200: "If we only listened with..."

#255: "We know more than we know we know."

#280: "To seduce almost anyone..."

#358: "It's not what you say..."

Love

#6: "Our job is the excuse..."

#70: "Love the giver more than the gift."

#92: "When love and skill work together..."

#127: "Ultimately the measure of every..."

#323: "The best use of life is love..."

#342: "The man is a success..."

Meaning

#1: "Your vision will become clear..."

#78: "To finish the moment..."

#154: "Yesterday is history..."

#197: "Enjoy the little things..."

#206: "I long to accomplish..."

Opportunities

#50: "When one door closes, another..."

#210: "A pessimist sees the..."

#238: "It is better to be prepared for..."

Optimism

#203: "Perpetual optimism..."

#210: "A pessimist sees the..."

#287: "The optimist already sees..."

#301: "Optimism is the faith that..."

#360: "Finish each day and be done..."

Passion

#20: "Do not wish to be anything..."

#56: "Life is playfulness. We need to..."

#62: "Don't ask yourself what the..."

#66: "Is the juice worth the squeezing?"

#121: "Adversity reveals genius..."

#129: "Become so wrapped up in something..."

#143: "To business that we love we rise bedtime..."

#144: "You have to have your heart in..."

#173: "Persistence prevails when all else fails."

#202: "Do not follow where the path..."

#248: "The mind is not a vessel..."

#269: "Only dead fish swim with..."

#270: "A man who works with his hands..."

#279: "To do what you love..."

#293: "I am seeking, I am striving..."

#316: "The race will go to..."

#325: "Do what you love and..."

#353: "Passion is energy..."

Patience

#212: "Have patience. All things are difficult..."

#341: "For fast acting relief..."

Peace

#11: "God, grant me the serenity..."

#68: "If you do everything calmly..."

#171: "Find inner peace and thousands..."

#253: "An eye for an eye will..."

#338: "Holding onto anger..."

Persistence

#8: "The hallmark of excellence..."

#33: "In the confrontation between..."

#40: "It's not what we eat but..."

#75: "Don't judge each day by..."

#120: "Genius does take shortcuts..."

#128: "Our greatest glory consists not in..."

#157: "Keep knocking and the joy inside..."

#173: "Persistence prevails when all else fails."

#174: "The race is not always to the swift..."

#259: "The journey of a thousand miles..."

#309: "People often say that motivation..."

#343: "No one would ever have..."

Perspective

#34: "It isn't the mountains..."

#42: "Change the way you look..."

#53: "Do what you know is right..."

#67: "Friendship is a soul dwelling..."

#103: "Success is a journey, not a destination."

#124: "The real voyage of discovery..."

#192: "At least three times a day..."

#203: "Perpetual optimism..."

#205: "Time is the coin of..."

#210: "A pessimist sees the..."

#344: "Look at everything as though..."

#349: "Kindred spirits are not so scarce..."

Playfulness

#49: "To succeed in life, you need..."

#56: "Life is playfulness. We need to..."

#76: "The master in the art of living..."

#84: "Life is about not knowing..."

#195: "Laughter is an instant vacation."

#247: "Genius is no more than..."

Possibilities

#26: "When I let go of what I am..."

#63: "There are powers inside of you..."

#199: "The ability to perceive..."

#210: "A pessimist sees the..."

#217: "A possibility is a hint..."

#266: "How do I work? I grope."

#330: "As your consciousness expands..."

#350: "You stand at a boundary..."

#360: "Finish each day and be done..."

Potential

#63: "There are powers inside of you..."

#164: "We are capable of greater things..."

#183: "The most exciting breakthroughs..."

#218: "If you won't be better tomorrow..."

#222: "The potential that exists within us..."

#285: "Problems are in your life..."

#346: "Teaching is an instinctual art..."

Progress

#15: "The greatest good you..."

#34: "It isn't the mountains..."

#37: "There is nothing noble in..."

#52: "Progress is impossible without..."

#60: "To raise new questions..."

#90: "Discontent is the first step..."

#139: "When you are tough on yourself..."

#145: "No one ever won a chess game by..."

#262: "Don't fight forces: use them."

#267: "How am I doing?"

Purpose

#27: "A man should conceive of..."

#29: "The best way to find..."

#179: "Good, better, best. Never let it rest..."

#190: "Nothing contributes so much..."

#202: "Do not follow where the path..."

#206: "I long to accomplish..."

#304: "Lighthouses don't go running..."

#337: "Live neither in the past nor..."

Quality

#35: "And in the end, it's not..."

#111: "Quality is never an accident..."

#117: "The quality of a person's life is..."

#189: "The universe will fill your cup..."

Reading

#185: "Reading one book is like..."

#186: "The unfed mind devours itself."

#208: "A man only learns in..."

#240: "A single conversation with a wise man..."

#265: "Great minds like a think."

#364: "The true university of these days..."

Relationships

#13: "The most important single..."

#23: "Keep away from people who..."

#24: "Kind words can be short..."

#28: "As human beings, our job..."

#32: "You can't help someone..."

#36: "If I am walking with two..."

#39: "Go to the people..."

#45: "Be who you are and say..."

#57: "If you go looking..."

#67: "Friendship is a soul dwelling..."

#70: "Love the giver more than the gift."

#85: "In everyone's life, at some time..."

#91: "That man is the richest whose..."

#115: "Our chief want in life is somebody..."

#118: "People seldom improve when they..."

#127: "Ultimately the measure of every..."

#135: "Behind every able man..."

Riches

#15: "The greatest good you..."

#28: "As human beings, our job..."

#55: "The work will wait while you show..."

#64: "Be thankful for what you have..."

#91: "That man is the richest whose..."

#182: "The highest reward for a person's toil..."

#201: "The best things in life..."

#220: "It is by spending oneself..."

#239: "Your network is your net worth."

#333: "No man becomes rich..."

Risk

#21: "Nothing ventured..."

#57: "If you go looking for a friend..."

#99: "Don't be afraid to go out..."

#204: "The greater danger for..."

#207: "We build too many walls..."

#264: "Try something different..."

#294: "I believe in getting into..."

Self-Discovery

#1: "Your vision will become clear..."

#10: "Every problem introduces..."

#29: "The best way to find..."

#122: "Of all knowledge, the wise and good..."

#130: "Act so as to elicit the best in others..."

#138: "Entrepreneurship is the last refuge..."

#171: "Find inner peace and thousands..."

#232: "To keep a lamp burning..."

#243: "Try to be like the turtle..."

#254: "We are betrayed by what is false within."

#260: "Choose yourself."

#275: "There's no greater power..."

#293: "I am seeking, I am striving..."

#296: "A man travels the world over..."

#303: "We forfeit three-quarters..."

Service

#29: "The best way to find..."

#77: "Life's most persistent and urgent question..."

#82: "The ultimate test of a man's conscience..."

#151: "No person was ever honored..."

#159: "Life is short. Do not forget about..."

#180: "Do your little bit of good wherever..."

#194: "Courage does not always roar..."

#231: "The heart that gives, gathers."

#257: "You can rest assured that if you..."

#268: "When you're presented with the opportunity..."

#304: "Lighthouses don't go running..."

#333: "No man becomes rich..."

Strength

#132: "The human spirit is stronger than..."

#246: "The first to apologize is..."

#340: "After climbing a great hill..."

Success

#3: "People are anxious to improve..."

#9: "Success in life comes not from..."

#13: "The most important single..."

#49: "To succeed in life, you need..."

#94: "Make happy those who are near..."

#98: "There are no shortcuts to..."

#103: "Success is a journey, not a destination."

#119: "Far better it is to dare mighty things..."

#137: "You read a book from beginning..."

#146: "I don't measure a man's success..."

#169: "A successful man is one who..."

#175: "The foundation stones for..."

#204: "The greater danger for..."

#212: "Have patience. All things are difficult..."

#244: "The great secret of success..."

#248: "The mind is not a vessel..."

#258: "Always bear in mind that your own..."

#276: "If a man does his best..."

#342: "The man is a success..."

Teamwork

#104: "Teamwork is the ability to work..."

#135: "Behind every able man..."

#142: "You can employ men and hire hands..."

#148: "Great men are rarely isolated..."

#167: "I have yet to find the man..."

#226: "There ain't no rules around here…"

#228: "A 'coach' remains something or someone who…"

#261: "Discipline is the bridge between…"

#274: "I not only use the brains I have…"

Thinking

#5: "Don't stumble over something…"

#38: "Not everything that is faced…"

#51: "When at a conflict between…"

#79: "Creativity involves breaking out…"

#83: "There is nothing either good or bad…"

#86: "It has been my observation that people…"

#93: "Rules and models destroy…"

#101: "One's mind, once stretched by a new idea…"

#107: "The environment you fashion…"

#158: "Life is all about choices…"

#164: "We are capable of greater things…"

#186: "The unfed mind devours itself."

#199: "The ability to perceive…"

#213: "Follow effective action with…"

#222: "The potential that exists within us…"

#223: "All meaningful and lasting change..."

#236: "I have lived a long life and..."

#245: "It's on the strength of observation..."

#255: "We know more than we know we know."

#265: "Great minds like a think."

#272: "One thought driven home..."

#274: "I not only use the brains I have..."

#312: "All words are pegs..."

#327: "Don't think *of* your goals..."

#328: "Our brains become magnetized..."

#329: "Think before you speak..."

Time

#4: "It's not what you've got..."

#35: "And in the end, it's not..."

#81: "The bad news is time flies..."

#183: "The most exciting breakthroughs..."

#205: "Time is the coin of..."

#302: "The price of anything..."

#323: "The best use of life is love..."

#363: "There are people whose clocks..."

Values

#45: "Be who you are and say..."

#51: "When at a conflict between..."

#77: "Life's most persistent and urgent question..."

#83: "There is nothing either good or bad..."

#140: "Goodwill is the one and only asset..."

#191: "Happiness is a state of consciousness..."

#192: "At least three times a day..."

#221: "An uneasy conscience is..."

#241: "If you can tell me who..."

#249: "The merit of originality..."

#279: "To do what you love..."

#286: "The world has a habit..."

#307: "Don't compromise yourself..."

Vision

#1: "Your vision will become clear..."

#27: "A man should conceive of..."

#43: "You cannot dream yourself..."

#44: "Learn from yesterday..."

#48: "Nothing happens unless first..."

#61: "Whatever you vividly imagine..."

#99: "Don't be afraid to go out..."

#133: "There are some people who live..."

#172: "Cherish your visions and..."

#202: "Do not follow where the path..."

#204: "The greater danger for..."

#217: "A possibility is a hint..."

#249: "The merit of originality..."

#252: "Dream big, but allow yourself..."

#321: "Dreams are powerful..."

#334: "I never hit a shot..."

#356: "Your greatness is..."

Wisdom

#7: "The wise man questions himself..."

#78: "To finish the moment..."

#87: "The way of a fool is right..."

#111: "Quality is never an accident..."

#114: "It's what you learn after you..."

#122: "Of all knowledge, the wise and good..."

#181: "People don't buy for logical reasons..."

#224: "One's first step in wisdom is to..."

#240: "A single conversation with a wise man..."

#271: "A prudent question is one-half of wisdom."

#281: "When it comes to life..."

#306: "The heart should be cultivated..."

#326: "Live your truth. Express your love..."

Words

#24: "Kind words can be short..."

#46: "You cannot talk your way out..."

#113: "Well done is better than well said."

#250: "We write to taste life twice..."

#283: "Words are small shapes in..."

#306: "The heart should be cultivated..."

#312: "All words are pegs..."

#329: "Think before you speak..."

#365: "Quotable quotes are..."

Work

#6: "Our job is the excuse..."

#18: "I firmly believe that any..."

#62: "Don't ask yourself what the..."

#76: "The master in the art of living..."

#80: "No one who rises before dawn..."

#123: "There is no medicine like hope..."

#136: "I know of no more encouraging fact..."

#138: "Entrepreneurship is the last refuge..."

#141: "The employer generally gets..."

#142: "You can employ men and hire hands..."

#143: "To business that we love we rise bedtime..."

#180: "Do your little bit of good wherever..."

#184: "Hard work without talent is a shame..."

#266: "How do I work? I grope."

#270: "A man who works with his hands..."

#279: "To do what you love..."

#282: "There can be no joy..."

#325: "Do what you love and..."

#353: "Passion is energy..."

45169546R00232

Made in the USA
Lexington, KY
18 September 2015